Praise for *Not a Happy Camper:*

"This book's success is a credit to the author's artful ability to combine her own sarcastic wit as a writer with the authentic voice of a naïve, yet perceptive, thirteen-year-old." —*Jewish Book World*

"Mindy Schneider [writes] with photographic precision and pungent Jewish humor." —Barbara Bamberger Scott, Bookreporter.com

"A delightful memoir. You needn't have attended sleepaway camp to appreciate Mindy Schneider's book. If you've ever left home, wondering who you really were and searching for a place to belong, this will resonate with you." —*Capital Region Living Magazine*

"In *Not a Happy Camper*, Mindy Schneider hilariously recalls her time at Kin-A-Hurra, an eight-week kosher summer camp in Maine that she attended in the 1970s. . . . Unlike many other memoirists these days, Ms. Schneider has no apparent desire to offer a tale of struggle and redemption or to search through her youth for the kernels of adult neurosis. She 'merely' draws a funny portrait of her younger self in a summer setting that anyone who has ever drunk bug juice will cringingly recognize."

—Kate Flatley LaVoie, *The Wall Street Journal*

"Something's not kosher at Camp Kin-A-Hurra and it's more than cheese in the beef stew. *Not a Happy Camper* is funnier than Laugh-A-Belly with your favorite bunkmates." —Patricia Volk, author of *Stuffed: Adventures of a Restaurant Family* and *To My Dearest Friends*

"The quick-wit of Schneider functions as a kind of life preserver, pulling the traditional tale from the bottom of the murky lake and adding an insightful clarity. . . . Expect to be entertained." —Bookslut.com

"*Not a Happy Camper* is a delightfully timeless reflection on a fleeting season in everyone's life. It dredged up my own repressed and awkward summer camp memories and somehow made them hilarious and bittersweet. Mindy Schneider deserves a tiara made out of macaroni and bits of yarn."

——Josh Kilmer-Purcell, author of *I Am Not Myself These Days*

"Mindy Schneider's summer as a thirteen-year-old at Camp Kin-A-Hurra is equal parts Ken Kesey and David Sedaris, a vivid and hilarious recapturing of adolescence through the eyes of a marvelous writer. I laughed my fool head off. What a kinahurra!" —Wendy Werris, author of *An Alphabetical Life*

"Ms. Schneider writes with a light, loving touch. . . . [A] must read." —*Jewish Times* (Baltimore)

Not a Happy Camper

Not a

Happy Camper

A MEMOIR

Mindy Schneider

Grove Press
New York

Published simultaneously in Canada
Printed in the United States of America

FIRST EDITION

Library of Congress Cataloging-in-Publication Data

Schneider, Mindy.
    Not a happy camper / by Mindy Schneider.
        p. cm.
    ISBN-13: 978-0-8021-4369-3
    ISBN-10: 0-8021-4369-5
    1. Schneider, Mindy—Childhood and youth.   2. Teenagers—Maine—
Biography.   3. Camps—Maine.   4. Maine—Biography.   I. Title.
    CT275.S34472A3 2007
    974.1'043092—dc22
    [B]
                                                        2006041280

Grove Press
an imprint of Grove/Atlantic, Inc.
841 Broadway
New York, NY 10003

Distributed by Publishers Group West

www.groveatlantic.com

08 09 10 11 12   10 9 8 7 6 5 4 3 2 1

Quiet, please!
Dedicated to the dining room

A Note to the Reader

I once went to a summer camp in Maine
that was not exactly what it was advertised to be.
For the sake of clarity in storytelling, I've altered
the chronology of certain events, changed some names, and
combined several people into each of the characters.

But this is how I remember it.

Not a Happy Camper

"We've got a cartload of Mindys."

Saul Rattner, camp director

Start here

I GREW UP IN THE 1970s, WHICH IS TO SAY I GREW UP REGRETTING the fact that I hadn't been born about ten years earlier. For those of us who became teenagers in 1974, our memories are not of Vietnam War protests, Woodstock, and the Summer of Love. If we recall anything at all, it's Watergate, gas rationing, and the early works of Barry Manilow. In my case, eight weeks at a summer camp in Maine with just one thing on my mind.

How vividly I can still remember standing by the edge of the lake, watching the Wolverines' cabin burn to the ground and thinking to myself, "Maybe this will be the summer I finally get a boyfriend." But I didn't want one of those boys from the Wolverines. First of all, I was thirteen and they were only twelve and, besides, they were kind of dumb, going along with Todd Zimmerman's plan to place lit candles under their beds before dinner so that by nightfall their sheets would be toasty warm. Though Todd and his bunkmates would grow up to be doctors, lawyers, college professors, and temporary dotcom moguls, all I saw that summer was a bunch of budding pyromaniacs. With their bunk a total loss, the Wolverines were split up and forced to spend the summer of 1974 living with the waiters over the boys' dining hall in rooms so hot you could bake muffins in the drawers, their quest for warmth fulfilled. My quest, on the other hand, was only just beginning.

1

I couldn't wait to go to sleepaway camp. I'd dreamed about it for years: the many wonderful friends I'd make, the one special boy I'd meet, the magical memories that would linger for a lifetime.

When I'd turned eleven, my parents said I was ready. But first they had to argue about it. My mother always wanted me to go to Camp Mohaph, where she'd spent her summers in the 1940s. Mohaph (not really an Indian word but an amalgam of the owners' names: Moe, Harry, and Phil) was a ritzy place populated by the children of Revlon cosmetics and Horowitz-Margareten kosher foods. My mother wasn't from quite as affluent a background, but her family owned a dry goods store on the Lower East Side so she had more underpants than anyone else. My father's experience was modest by comparison. He went to Boy Scout camp for only a week, sleeping outdoors in a tent and swimming in an itchy wool bathing suit his mother knitted for him. After serving in the navy during World War II (and successfully defending Annapolis, Maryland), my father was hired by beautiful Camp Cicada in the Catskill Mountains, where he was voted Most Popular Counselor.

"Why can't Mindy go to Mohaph?" my mother questioned.

"Because she's going to Cicada," my father answered.

"But you promised when I was pregnant that our kids would go to *my* camp!"

"You were making me nuts," he reminded her. "I'd have said yes to anything."

It didn't matter to me who won. I just wanted to go to camp. In the end my father prevailed and, for my first summer away from home, I went to his alma mater, but only because Mohaph had recently gone out of business. As it turned out, I didn't enjoy my summer at Cicada.

"The girls were really mean," I told my parents.

"I'm sure they were just shy," my mother insisted.

"And they're all really rich and have nicer clothes than me and the counselors make you fold your blankets a certain way and I couldn't do it."

"I loved my summers at Cicada," my father reminisced. "I think you should give it another try."

When I disliked it even more the second year, I told my parents they were wasting their money. This did the trick, and they agreed I could pick any camp in the entire country to attend the following summer, as long as it had a kosher kitchen. I had three choices.

We met with the owners of two of the camps, also located in the Catskills, but both places looked and sounded like the rigid, snobby nightmare I'd just fled. Then there was Camp Kin-A-Hurra in Maine, the Vacationland state. Owner/director Saul Rattner scheduled an appointment at our house in Springfield, New Jersey, in the winter of 1973. Maine sounded so far away and exotic that the thought of Saul's visit filled me with nervous expectation. I waited in the den, watching a rerun of *My Three Sons*, wondering how so many people could live in one house and still stay calm.

My mother was in the kitchen, removing the plastic floral centerpiece from the table, when the doorbell rang. My father got up to answer, motioning for me to turn off the TV and for my brothers to go upstairs. I stood ten feet away as a pipe-smoking, mellow-voiced man in his fifties crossed our threshold, greeting my father with a hearty handshake, the kind where you use both hands. "Wonderful to meet you," he said, sounding like he genuinely meant it.

Saul spoke with the quiet authority of a rabbi, though he was dressed in khaki pants and a safari vest and he drove a jeep, as if he'd needed a machete to cut through the brush to reach our tract house in the suburbs. I couldn't tell if my parents looked comfortable or skeptical as my father led this stranger into our kitchen. When he heard my name, Saul smiled and said, "Oh yes, we've got a cartload of Mindys." I chose to interpret this as his way of calling me ordinary.

Nevertheless, I was thrilled when he took a seat at our white lacquer-look table with the turquoise vinyl chairs and backed up his sales pitch with photographs of a beautifully maintained wooded paradise blessed with endless golden sunshine.

"Archery, arts and crafts, all the usual activities," Saul explained, waving his pipe across the glossy black and white images in the catalog. "Plus we take the campers on lots of wonderful trips. Mountain climbing, canoeing. Our campers come from all around the world and we feel it's our duty to show off the magnificence of Maine. It's quite exquisite."

"Must get pretty cold at night," my father said.

"That's why the bunks are heated," Saul replied.

"Really?" my mother asked. "Never heard of a camp having that."

"Oh, it's essential," he assured her.

"What's this?" I asked, pointing at the next page.

"That's a camper developing pictures in our photo lab," Saul explained. "Do you like photography? Do you own a camera?"

"Yeah! I do! They were giving them away for free at the Esso station when it changed over to Exxon, so we filled up both cars so we could get two cameras, even though my mother's car only needed like a dollar's worth."

"Uh, that's enough," my father cut in.

But it wasn't enough. I wanted more. I wanted to go to this camp with the kids from all over the world, go canoeing with them and learn photography and come home with snapshots like the ones in Saul's catalog. This was the place for me.

"You really don't want to go to one of these camps in New York?" my mother asked. "It's so much closer."

"I don't know," I said. "They just looked . . . the same."

"And the one in Maine?"

"Looked . . . different."

I was thirteen years old and I knew what I wanted. This time the choice would be mine. All my parents had to do was pay for it.

In the 1970s, an eight-week stay at a privately owned camp cost an astronomical twelve hundred dollars. Eleven-fifty if you registered early. I didn't know how my father was able to afford this. My older brother, Mark, and I have often discussed the fact that up until we graduated from college and our parents built a new house—the biggest one in town—we believed our family was extremely poor.

My father had often spent nights and weekends at his family's grocery store in Jersey City. One time, when Mark was five years old, a neighbor asked him what our father did for a living and Mark said, "My daddy's a delivery boy." I knew he was also a lawyer, but even so it seemed money was always tight. It was surprising that for a third summer in a row my parents could afford to send me to camp. It was not surprising, however, that they decided to save on airfare by driving me there.

My father loved to drive. He would take our family anywhere, so long as we could reach it by car. His family had worked seven days a week and never owned one, never traveled. Growing up, he'd been denied the opportunity to revel in motorized family togetherness.

Both of my parents enjoyed visiting Colonial restorations so we spent our vacations watching women in old-fashioned bonnets demonstrate candle dipping while our friends' families vacationed in Florida. They came back with tans. We came back with brochures. No matter how far away some historic site might be, we'd pile into the olive green and faux wood-paneled Oldsmobile Custom Cruiser and drive.

As it was, my father was the only one who loved these road trips. My middle brother, Jay, who would go on to become a renowned paleontologist and the world's foremost authority on giant mollusks, suffered terribly from motion sickness. Jay threw up everywhere. In a futile attempt to control the vomiting, Jay was always seated next to a window. As a result, our family trips became a series of backseat arguments with my older brother Mark and I fighting over who got the other window and who got smushed in the middle seat with the hump on the floor and no legroom, next to barfing Jay. It didn't help that my father would tune the radio to WVNJoy, a station that made elevator music sound hip.

That summer, in late June of 1974, I had the entire backseat to myself. My brothers stayed home with my grandmother while I rode with my parents northward to my destiny. It might have been a pleasant trip, but my father had no sense of direction and my mother had no sense of how loud her voice could get. These were my parents. They spent a day and a half screaming over the Muzak about the road signs as my mother tried to figure out the Auto Club TripTik.

"Mom, you always liked camp, right?" I asked as we made another U-turn to undo another wrong turn.

"Sure," she said. "We didn't have air-conditioning. It was much cooler than the city."

I knew she'd liked it for another reason: she'd had a boyfriend at camp. I never asked my mother about her dating history, but she'd told me anyway, at my grandmother's house in Brooklyn, when I came across an old scrapbook.

"Oh, look, that's Boris Kazikoff," she said. "He took me to the movies, to see Bing Crosby in *Going My Way*, and tried to get fresh by putting his arm around me in the dark."

That was her first date. When she ditched Boris for summer camp, she met someone she liked better.

"Mohaph had weekly boy-girl dances," my mother told me. "I was afraid no one would ask me to dance because I was so skinny. Then, at the first dance, this nice, cute boy started talking to me. We danced together every week that whole summer. I can't remember his name . . ."

He was her first boyfriend and she was only twelve. I was already a year behind my mother.

Somewhere around Portsmouth, New Hampshire, we got so lost that my father had to pull off the highway and ask for directions at an antiques shop. There, my mother spotted an eighteenth-century grandfather clock, exactly the kind she'd been longing for, but with me and my trunk and duffel bag there wasn't enough room for it in the car. We got our bearings, but not the clock, and continued on our way.

When we finally arrived in Canaan, Maine, and pulled into the camp, my heart sank. It looked nothing like the pictures. Saul had shown us photographs of an inviting sunny place, all chipper, bright, and freshly painted—the kind of camp Walt Disney or the residents of Oz might have sent their kids to, if they'd been Jewish. The shabby little buildings of Camp Kin-A-Hurra, with their peeling paint and sagging rooflines, made the Colonial homes my family toured—the ones held together with sticks and mud and a wing and a prayer—look like palaces. I'd built better-looking structures with my brothers' Lincoln Logs. We'd been duped. *I'd* been duped and I'd convinced my parents to fall for the scam. I wanted to turn around and go home, but I couldn't. I could never live this down. I wanted to say something, but I didn't dare because I knew what the response would be.

"You picked this camp," my mother would say sharply. "We drove you all the way here."

My father would add, "You could've gone back to Cicada. Now it's too late."

My parents had done this nice thing for me. I owed it to them to keep quiet and be miserable. I couldn't even look at them, which is why I only recently learned that my parents had had the same unsettling first impression. But they weren't about to lose their deposit and lug me and all of my belongings back to the Garden State. Instead, my father gave me a dollar for spending money, which, even back in the early seventies, was worth next to nothing.

On the way home, amidst what was no doubt another day and a half of screaming, they got lost in the exact same place, pulled off the highway to get directions, and bought that grandfather clock for six hundred dollars, easily loading it into the now empty back of the wagon. My mother recently had it appraised and today the clock is worth twelve thousand dollars. Over the years, my parents also acquired two banjo clocks, a Swiss cuckoo, and a mantel clock. Thus, in addition to all the yelling and screaming, every fifteen minutes the whole house chimed and bonged.

The other campers' parents had sprung for airfare and the girls hadn't yet arrived from the airport. I was the first one in Bunk Three, just me and my counselor, the very redheaded Gita Isak. I wished I had red hair. People remember you.

Before leaving, my mother had helped me pick out "a good bed," one with a newer foam mattress covered in vinyl. Unlike the old, stuffed blue-and-white ticking-stripe mattresses, the slick newer ones repelled unwanted liquids. On the downside, they also made the sheets slide off. "Still," my mother said, "it's the better choice, I think." Now I was sitting on it, wondering what to do with myself and how I could make this summer better than the last two. I felt a little bit sad but couldn't put my finger on why. Homesickness didn't seem right, especially since my parents weren't even at home. They were still on the road somewhere, probably yelling.

Whenever I couldn't understand what I was feeling, my mother would tell me I was "going through a phase." This drove me crazy, as if she perceived me as just a series of clichés and not as an actual person. I did not want to be going through this "phase" at camp, so I needed to find a distraction. I took out my clarinet and began to practice.

My father was convinced it was important for me to play a musical instrument. I'd need all the help I could get, all the extracurricular activities I could muster, to include on my college applications. The clarinet was a very practical choice. You could play it in both a concert band and a marching band. Even if you sucked, like I did. I am certain that throughout the 1970s and '80s, America's Ivy League colleges were populated with smart but wretched clarinet players.

If I'd been the least bit talented, breaking out my instrument on my first day in Bunk Three would still have been bizarre behavior. It certainly caught Gita Isak's attention that day.

"Mindy?"

I put down the clarinet. "Uh-huh."

"Why don't you hold off unpacking your trunk . . ."

"And just keep playing?"

"Maybe hold off on that, too."

Then she left the bunk. Not a music lover, I surmised. Gita returned a few minutes later with another counselor, the Twiggy-thin Madeline Rattner, who was the camp owner's fourth cousin twice removed, and the three of us had a little talk.

"You know, you're . . . very mature," Gita pointed out.

I liked where this appeared to be going.

"So we're thinking you might be happier next door in Bunk Two," Maddy said. "My bunk. The girls are a little more mature."

I took this comment as a compliment, believing perhaps "maturity" referred to my fine appreciation of music and general grown-upness and that this was good. Mature girls got boyfriends.

My new bunkmates arrived from the Bangor Airport a couple of hours later. There were four of them, two old-timers and two newcomers like me. I tried to size them all up, see if any were as mature as I. That first evening, as we finished shoving our clothes into the splintery cubbyholes along the back wall and scratching the first of many mosquito bites to come, I asked about the paneled, heated accommodations Saul had described when he sat in my kitchen.

"He told you about those, too?" newcomer Betty Gilbert asked. Betty had filled an entire cubbyhole with books. I figured she either read a lot or had flunked a class in school and had to make it up over the summer.

Dana Bleckman, back for her fifth season, filled us in on the camp's owner. "Okay, there's one thing you need to know about Saul," she said, laughing. "He's a big fat liar. Everything he says is a lie. There's no paneled, heated bunks, no fruit cart that comes around before bedtime, no private camp-owned hydroplane. And just ask

Max Peretz—who showed up for his first summer with a brand-new set of clubs—no Camp Kin-A-Hurra nine-hole golf course."

"What about Golda Meir and Moshe Dayan?" I asked.

"Sorry," Dana said. "They were never counselors here."

"That's a new one," piped in the other returning camper, the hip, hot pants–wearing Autumn Evening Schwartz.

"No, he tried that one on me, too," Dana continued. "Said Golda Meir ran Girls' Side and Moshe Dayan taught archery. Like anyone would buy that."

Actually, I had. It explained Mr. Dayan's eye and all. I glanced over at the third new girl in my bunk, Hallie Susser, and the look on her face told me she'd believed it, too.

The conversation shifted when Dana did something I could only dream of doing; she pulled out a guitar and started to play. Dana was one of those people a summer camp can't exist without. A singer and a composer, she had even performed on TV, although it was only UHF. Dana strummed a few chords and hummed softly while the rest of us pulled everything back out of our cubbyholes, looking for pajamas. Talented and beautiful, Dana was pretty much what I wished I was and feared—okay, knew—I wasn't. One of those girls who always got a boyfriend.

That night, before bed, I wanted to use the bathroom and brush my teeth before climbing into my cot under the scratchy green wool army surplus blankets my mother had taken to her summer camp thirty years before. One little problem. The toilet in our bunk wasn't working. "Find your raincoats and your flashlights, girls," Maddy instructed us after inspecting the unusable facility. "We'll try the bunk next door."

Maddy had spent fifteen of her twenty summers here and refused to speak ill of her distant relative. Whenever someone ques-

tioned her about Saul's fantastic stories and outrageous claims, she
got this sort of faraway glazed look in her eyes, like she couldn't
see or hear what you were saying. Maddy was studying classics at
Amherst College, but her real goal in life was keeping off the weight
she'd recently lost. During the spring semester she'd contracted
dysentery, which she described as "the best disease I ever had," and
dropped twenty-two pounds. Now, at five-six and one hundred and
five pounds, she was way too thin, which, in her mind, equaled
good. To keep the weight off, Maddy had come to camp with a
little brown suitcase filled with the staples of her new diet. I peeked
in once.

"That's what you eat?" I asked her. "Pep-O-Mint Lifesavers and
salted soybeans?"

"I exercise, too," was all Maddy said, closing the lid as if she
feared I might steal her stash.

A seasoned camper, Maddy had also brought along several extra
rain ponchos and flashlights, as she had a tendency to lose these
items and both were crucial to a summer at Kin-A-Hurra. Apparently, summer was the official rainy season in this part of Maine,
along with spring and fall. In the winter it just snowed.

Now, she led us out the front door and into the downpour on
an expedition to Bunk One. Its plumbing was broken as well.

"We were planning on coming to your bunk," one of the girls
at Bunk One informed us.

"This is a disaster," my bunkmate Betty groaned.

Yes, it was, one that I wouldn't write home to my parents about
because I was sure they'd somehow blame me.

"The toilets at Cicada always worked," I was certain they'd write
back.

"Let's try another bunk," Maddy suggested.

Sometimes the nice thing about being in a disaster is not being in it alone. Campers and counselors from several other bunks

joined our group and we became a massive horde of rubberized yellow trudging around in the mud. We learned that none of the bunks had working facilities. Our only hope was the girls' dining hall, the Point.

Built on a peninsula jutting out into the middle of the lake, the Point had been built in 1907, back when this property had been a hunting lodge. A truly beautiful building, it featured peg-and-groove hardwood floors, knotty pine paneling, and a massive stone fireplace—and the original overhead pull-chain toilets, but at least they were working. There were three bathroom stalls and eighty-five of us. After waiting in the hallway for half an hour, and learning the words to an uncomplimentary camp song, I decided I could hold off using the bathroom until morning, a skill that would serve me well for the remainder of the summer.

Just outside the Point, a cluster of girls stood by the shore, watching a structure across the lake, over on Boys' Side, go up in flames in spite of the inclement weather.

I feared it was one of the bunks. Specifically, I feared it was the thirteen-year-old boys' bunk and that someone would die. The boy who was perfect for me, the one I was supposed to date. The one I was supposed to marry in ten years. I hadn't even met him yet and now everything was ruined.

The blare of the fire engine's siren echoed across the lake.

"Oh my God! The whole camp's burning down!" one girl cried out.

"No, I think it's just a bunk. Hope no one's inside," another girl said.

"Looks like the Wolverines' bunk," someone else called out as the fire department's truck roared into view.

"How old are the Wolverines?" I asked.

"Eleven and twelve," came the answer. "Why?"

"Uh—no reason," I insisted.

I stood with the other girls and watched as the fire was put out, but my mind was already leaping ahead to the next catastrophe. We'd just lost the plumbing. Would the electricity go out, too? If so, would my flashlight batteries last eight weeks? And if not—wait—that could be a good thing. I knew all about the days before electricity. I could show everyone how to survive this summer. I could demonstrate how to dip wicks into hot wax and maybe everyone would think I was really cool. Maybe this would be the road to my salvation, my path to popularity.

Maybe this was how I'd get a boyfriend.

Or maybe everyone would think I was just some oddball who knew way too much about candles.

to the tune of
"O Come, All Ye Faithful"

"O come to Kin-A-Hurra
Come get hepatitis
Mononucleosis and diarrhea, too
Come if you're nuts
Come if you're a klutz
The summer will go by
As fast as turtles fly
We'll be here till we die
Saul, why're we here?"

2

At my old camp, Camp Cicada, the third period of each day was reserved for General Swim. I hated General Swim. The Girls' Waterfront was marked off in four sections: Sharks, Perch, Minnows, and Guppies. Most of the girls in my bunk were Sharks, having passed their deepwater tests. I was a Minnow, a twelve-year-old minnow, which wouldn't have been so bad if you didn't have to have a buddy, but you did, so I'd usually end up partnered with a six-year-old. You know that guy who said it's good to be a big fish in a small pond? I hated that guy almost as much as I hated General Swim.

The Camp Cicada girls' head counselor would wake us up every morning by playing a 45 rpm recording of reveille on a public address system. Then he would tell us the weather forecast and what we should wear to breakfast and pretty much everything else we'd be doing that day, each period demarcated by more recordings of army drill music as we lined up in front of our bunks and then marched single file to our next fun-filled activity. The camp had drawn up the schedule around 1952 and I'm pretty sure it never strayed. Even when it rained and we stayed indoors, orders were barked out over the PA system: now you'll write letters, now you'll wash the toilets, now you'll have quiet time . . .

The only thing we got to decide for ourselves was the order in which we'd shower each evening before dinner. As soon as we awakened to reveille, girls would pop up out of bed and shout, "First shower!" "Second shower!," etc., until everyone had a place in line, except me. I was always last because I never had the nerve to jump in and call out a number. I hoped things would be different—or at least *I* would be different—at Camp Kin-A-Hurra.

"This is not what I expected!"

That's what Betty Gilbert yelled out in her sleep and that's what I awoke to my first morning at camp.

"A sleep-talker! I love it!" whispered Autumn Evening Schwartz, awake now in her bed, two feet from mine.

There were six little army cots in our bunk, three on each side. We slept with our heads up against the wall, feet pointing toward the aisle. I would have expected our counselor to take a bed at the back of the bunk, for privacy. When I looked over I knew why she'd selected the one closest to the door. It was empty. Maddy had escaped in the middle of the night.

"You guys up?" It was Dana Bleckman. She stretched and took the ponytail holder out of her hair.

"Where's Maddy? I asked. "Think she went home?"

"Nah. Her stuff is still here. Maybe she went to the Point to use the bathroom. Maybe she'll meet us at breakfast."

"What do we do after breakfast?" asked Hallie Susser, who slept across the aisle from me.

"We come back to the bunk," Dana answered.

"And then what?" I asked. "Clean the bunk? Sweep the floor? What's the schedule?"

"Schedule?" Dana laughed. "We eat, we do stuff, we eat some more, we do some more stuff."

Autumn Evening yawned. "Like that."

Betty opened her eyes. "Could you guys keep it down? I'm trying to sleep."

For the first two days we sat indoors, reading comic books and playing jacks, as we listened to Top Forty hits on local radio station WSKW in Skowhegan. My father believed in library books and did not permit my brothers and me to spend our money on comics and magazines. At Camp Cicada, the other girls had them, but when I asked to borrow one the snooty response I got was, "And what will you give me?" It's not that the girls at Cicada didn't like me, or that they didn't like me for any good reason. It's just that I wasn't born and bred on Long Island like they were. I was an illegal alien and they refused to stamp my passport.

"Hey, wanna read my *Archie Joke Book*?" Dana asked, tossing it my way. Here, at last, I had my chance to catch up with the kids at Riverdale High, to read the latest movie spoof in *Mad* magazine, and to ogle open-shirt photos of Tony DeFranco in *Tiger Beat*. You'd think I couldn't ask for more, but then I did.

"What do we do when the rain stops?"

Autumn Evening thought a moment. "Um . . . this."

"That's not true," said Dana. "Sometimes we sit outside and read. And sometimes we go down to the beach."

It was so random and so free, and it seemed like everybody knew it. At other camps, we knew what we were supposed to be doing: the hours and hours of kickball, tennis, and swim instruction complemented by yarn crafts and nature walks and daily bunk inspections where neatness counted. But the schedule at Kin-A-Hurra was more like this: do anything you want anytime you want, unless you just want to do nothing. And so this was how the days were passed, except that the older girls also smoked cigarettes. In my search to find the perfect camp, I had landed instead at the anti-camp.

It was easy to like Kin-A-Hurra, if not for what it did have then for what it didn't. For instance, there was no public address system. In its place was an old ship's bell hanging from a decrepit flagpole. (The idea was to raise the American, Canadian, and Israeli flags, but so far we hadn't raised anything due to the rain.) Our dedicated head counselor, Wendy Katz, rang that bell every hour even though we never changed activities and there was no real need for her to keep getting wet. The old wooden bunks had sheet-metal roofs and the sound of the rain pounding down on them was almost deafening, but in a pleasant, reassuring way. On the hour, the conversation would become, "Was that the bell?" "Did you hear the bell?" "What time is it?" Somehow we always knew when it was time for a meal and we'd take a break from our minimal activity and head down to the dining hall.

The Point possessed a grace and serenity the rest of camp lacked. It was the one dry place where all of Girls' Side regularly assembled and our high-pitched voices sweetly filled the oversized lodge. This was most evident when we sang the blessing over the food, in Hebrew, before meals. I made it a habit to keep my voice low and listen to how perfect and harmonious everyone else sounded together.

Back home, we never thanked God before a meal. We never even thanked my mother. We just ate. My father was religious, yet he allowed us to sit down at the table and plow through the meal as fast as we could in order to get back to watching TV. My parents, seated at the two heads, rarely noticed just how quickly we ate. My father was absorbed in the *New York Times* crossword puzzle and my mother flipped through *House Beautiful* magazine. My three brothers and I were seated in between them on both sides of the table, squeezed together to make room for their reading material.

The one exception was Thanksgiving, which was always held at Aunt Judy's house in Jericho, Long Island, though not actually on Thanksgiving Day. Our family celebrated Thanksgiving the Saturday before because there was less traffic. As Uncle Hank finished carving the turkey with the electric knife he'd gotten from saving S&H Green Stamps, someone from my mother's side would shout out, "We forgot to make a blessing!" and we'd hurriedly say one, as if we feared God might be doing a spot check.

Meanwhile, Uncle Hank prattled on, showing off his vast knowledge of wine, which was meaningless to me as my entire frame of reference consisted of the words Manischewitz and concord grape. "Here, Tom," he said one time. (He called me Tom because I was a tomboy.) "Try this." Then he laughed as I nearly gagged on his latest overpriced merlot.

Thanksgiving at the relatives' was one of the few occasions when we ate out. My mother didn't like restaurants. She didn't like having to sit and wait. "If we were at home, we'd be done by now," she'd say impatiently, and then scold us for filling up on bread. My mother preferred to make the food herself and then act annoyed if my brothers and I didn't want to eat it. Once a month she'd make breaded flounder and once a month I'd practically cry, telling her how much I detested it. "Just eat it this once and I'll never make it again," my mother would tell me. I fell for that line for seventeen years.

"Ooh! Howard Johnson's! Can we stop there?" Howard Johnson's was the one restaurant my parents liked, bland and consistent with prompt service. Everyone but Jay loved to stop for food on the road. Lucky for me, both my mother and father had a sweet tooth and we especially enjoyed the ice cream sundaes, despite their shallow convex metal dishes, served with a little cookie on the side.

"No whipped cream or cherry on mine," my mother would tell the waitress. "I'm on a diet." My mother thought this was funny every single time.

Sometimes when we were on vacation we'd go to HoJo's for dinner and my father would let us order the Tom Turkey entrée from the children's menu, as if eating nonkosher turkey was somehow all right if it came with a paper placemat and crayons. But when we ate dinner there, we couldn't have sundaes for dessert. It isn't permissible to mix milk and meat and we'd have to settle for orange sherbet. That came with a little cookie, too, but it just wasn't the same. On very rare and fancy occasions we ate at Larry's Kosher Deli in Plainfield, New Jersey. When I was three years old and we went to the New York World's Fair, we brought our own tuna sandwiches from home. We never went to McDonald's. My father believed keeping kosher was an honor bestowed upon the Chosen People and my mother felt it was a worthy tradition, a way to acknowledge our ancestors. But to me it was a burden, something that set me apart from my peers and held me back, although the thought of eating any part of a pig still kind of grossed me out.

At Kin-A-Hurra, all of the meals for Girls' Side were prepared on Boys' Side, then trucked around the lake to be vaguely reheated, and they tasted like it. Still, I enjoyed eating in the Point. There was no need to impress anyone, no risk of being rejected. The Point was safe, our own private girls' world, no boys to worry about. And yet, I wasn't getting any younger . . .

Following three days of heavy rain, the weather cleared and it was finally time to go to the other side of the lake, to meet our counterparts, the Foxes. The boys. While the girls of Kin-A-Hurra may not have followed a set daily schedule, we most definitely had specific goals to achieve by summer's end. For the youngest campers, the nine-and-under crowd, this meant overcoming homesickness and learning to act casual when letters and packages arrived; for the ten- and eleven-year-olds, it was taking advantage of being away and selecting your own candy bars at the store or seeing who could make the most macramé bracelets; and for the twelve-year-olds it was all about looking good, about borrowing clothing and accessories from your friends and learning to blow-dry your hair straight despite the humidity because, once you turned thirteen, it was all about the boys.

I was thirteen. I didn't have to learn how to build a fire or construct an elaborate "God's eye" from yarn and twigs. The only thing I really had to do was get a boyfriend so I could have some-one to say good-bye to at the end. Someone to kiss good-bye. That was really what this summer was about, getting that first kiss by the last night of camp.

We had an hour after dinner to get ready for the trip across the lake. Back at the bunk, Autumn Evening pulled on superwide bell-bottom jeans, a peasant blouse, and a kerchief around her head that made her look like Rhoda. Autumn Evening was smart and cool and studied Jewish mysticism (whatever that was) along with all other forms of spirituality. She had tarot cards and a Ouija board and claimed she could get in touch with dead campers from the 1920s. I just wanted to connect with one of those still breathing across the lake.

It would have been nice to have clothes that flattered my ap-pearance, but my brothers and I grew up wearing hand-me-downs from Victor and Judy Horowitz. They apparently dressed like characters from the *Sally, Dick, and Jane* books. My parents had met Victor and Judy's parents in 1957 when both couples were honeymooning at a hotel in Dixville Notch, New Hampshire (from which my mother stole the hangers).

One time in geometry class, as I turned my protractor to mea-sure an angle, Billy Robertson, a bully who sat by the Rand McNally map of the world, called out, "Hey, look at that kid's pants!"

Billy pointed to a boy passing by in the hallway, dressed in corduroys too short at the bottom and too wide at the waist. The class burst out laughing and I joined in.

"Yeah, imagine what the rest of his family must look like," I said.

The boy out in the hall was my brother Jay.

At around age ten, when it became obvious that I was growing at a faster rate than Judy Horowitz, my mother bought me jeans at the local store, Rynette's, but always from the clearance rack. Tonight in Bunk Two, I pored over my Rynette's rejects, checking to see what the two other newcomers were doing. Betty was anal-retentive, but the term we used back then was "weird." Obsessed with keeping the contents of her cubbyholes tidy, Betty was determined to hate camp. She fumed about the weather, about the bunks, and about the food, and she marked off the days, prison-style, with a black felt-tip pen on the wall above her bed. Betty put on an Oxford button-down shirt and gym shorts and picked up the book she was reading, *Sybil*, so she could sit in a corner and ignore everyone once we got to Boys' Side. Betty Gilbert was the girl with no personality reading the book about the girl with sixteen. We hoped one might rub off.

Hallie, on the other hand, was trying as hard as I was. Hallie was tempted to wear the flouncy sky-blue polyester ball gown she was supposed to save for the Banquet Social in August.

"Should I wear this?" she asked me, holding it up.

"Well," I said, "you might get it dirty and then you couldn't wear it again at the end of the summer. 'Cause, y'know, I wouldn't send it out to the camp laundry."

Instead, Hallie and I took a cue from our counselor, a college girl, and wore flannel shirts, jeans, and clogs. We were as ready as we were going to be.

Most camps cart kids around in yellow school buses, but the ever enterprising Saul Rattner employed a more cost-effective system. Kin-A-Hurra owned a fleet of old broken-down vehicles and the six of us traveled to Boys' Side via the 1962 Plymouth Valiant. The light blue rust-encrusted car featured a steering wheel and a series of gaping holes with wires poking out from the remains of the dashboard. The vinyl top was shredded; Autumn Evening called it a moon roof. Saul had purchased this car for eighty dollars at a bankruptcy auction.

The Valiant had no brakes, not to mention shock absorbers, and the ride down the dirt road, back out to U.S. Route 2, was a bumpy one. When we reached the stone pillars and the wooden sign at the entrance that read "Camp Kin-A-Hurra for Girls," we turned left and drove two hundred feet down the highway. Another left took us into "Camp Kin-A-Hurra for Boys" and onto an even longer dirt road. We drove by a bunch of ramshackle cottages that did not look like bunks. Kids who did not look like campers were running around and playing. Adults who did not look like counselors were barbecuing and drinking beer and shooting us nasty looks as we drove past.

The explanation was simple. Due to a zoning glitch, a five-hundred-foot section of the only road leading to Boys' Side was not camp property. People from town owned the houses along this stretch of the lake known as the Public Beach. Though Camp Kin-A-Hurra was a private camp, the locals came and went constantly, summering right in the middle of it.

The longer I sat in that car, the more I worried this might be my third boyfriend-less summer in a row. I had reached five feet tall by the time I was ten and now, three years later, I towered over the boys at five-four (unaware back then that this would be my final adult height). I was not a beanpole, however. I weighed one hundred and twenty pounds (unaware this would *not* be my final adult weight). My one consolation was that my size and height drew attention away from the braces Dr. Gottlieb had chained to my teeth that year, and away from the nose I'd inherited from my mother's father.

Just before the entrance to Boys' Side, we passed a larger, beautiful wood shingle home, perfectly situated on the edge of the lake. Maddy slowed down as we drove by.

"This is my dream house," she said. "I've always wanted to live here."

"Maybe someday the owner will sell it to you," I offered.

"Maybe," Maddy smiled. "It's Saul's."

Kin-A-Hurra's Boys' Side was older, larger, and more spread out than ours. The first building we came upon was the Social Hall, a big square block from the early 1900s with a high-pitched roof and a stage at one end. That's where we met the Foxes.

At your first school dance—or your first bar mitzvah party— there is usually music and there is awkwardness. We didn't have any music. My bunkmates and I entered slowly, in a tight, giggly, nail-biting cluster. The eight Foxes, already inside, moved away, as if we were the plague or some evil apparition. They stopped only when their backs were literally up against the wall and then they stood there, wordlessly staring at us.

Only Autumn Evening was immediately comfortable and only because she didn't care. ("I've had boyfriends in all of my past lives," she'd explained earlier. "Frankly, I'm a little burnt out by men.")

Breaking free from the group, she announced, "Hello, Foxes! This is us. This is it. We're all you get this summer."

I wished I'd brought a book so I could join Betty, who quickly found a spot backstage in which to hide.

Maddy and the boys' counselor stood by the door, trying not to laugh at us as they motioned to our two groups to move closer together. After ten minutes of this agony, Maddy announced, "We'll see you guys a little later," and the two counselors left.

At Autumn Evening's suggestion, we all sat down in a circle. Dana struck up a conversation with the boy next to her, which made me think, *That's what I need to do. Talk to the boy next to me. Just chat like it's nothing. Like I'm an interesting person. Like I know I'm an interesting person. Like I'm doing him a favor talking to him. Hmmm. How does witty banter go?*

No need, though. The boy on my right looked past me and addressed Autumn Evening, interrupting her conversation with Philip Selig, a short, scrawny kid in a Mets baseball cap, the kind of boy I was trying not to notice.

The Fox I couldn't take my eyes off was Kenny Uber, seated across the circle. He was cute with wavy light brown hair and a rugged look about him, like he shopped at the army-navy store because he actually used the stuff. I pictured him fishing and hunting and conquering the land, the drawing on the far right of Darwin's Dream Jew chart. He was perfect.

"Let's hold a séance," Autumn Evening proposed.

"Who would we conjure up?" one of the boys wanted to know.

The votes were equally split among Bluebeard the pirate, Harry Houdini, and the guy who invented gum. Unable to reach a compromise, we decided instead to hold a levitation, gathering around a person, saying a bunch of mystical-sounding mumbo-jumbo, and lifting her high in the air.

Dana was chosen and lay down on the floor as ten of us crouched around her and placed our index and middle fingers under her body. I was directly across from Kenny, but he wasn't looking at me. I wanted to say hello or at least say something, but there was no time. Someone hit the lights. In the near pitch-blackness, Autumn Evening began the incantation. We went around the circle and repeated her words.

"She looks sick."

"She looks sick."

"She looks sick."

All of us solemnly repeated the words, like a mantra.

"She *is* sick."

"She *is* sick."

"She *is* sick"

And so forth.

After three more rounds of false observations, Autumn Evening whispered, "Let's lift her."

Dana's body rose in the air to our gasps of surprise and delight.

"It's really working!" Hallie shouted out.

"Shhh, you'll break the spell," Autumn Evening admonished.

"Oh, c'mon," said the skinny boy in the Mets cap. "There's ten of us. That's forty fingers holding up, like, what, ninety pounds?"

Dana herself appeared to be in a trance for several moments until she shouted out, "Put me down, I need to pee!"

We practically dropped her as the counselors returned, turning the lights back on and announcing it was time to leave. In an instant, the mood and the tension were broken, which was okay by me. I was pretty sure I'd made a good first impression on the boys. I hadn't done anything memorably stupid.

After a quick good night, my bunkmates and I were all safely jammed back inside the Valiant, clown car–style. Maddy put the key in the ignition, turned it, and—nothing. The engine was dead. Not even a cough or a sputter. We'd have to find another way back across the lake.

"What about the motorboat?" Autumn Evening suggested.

"I don't think so," Maddy said. "There's a lot of rocks in the lake. It's dangerous."

"Especially when Maddy's at the wheel," Dana added.

"It's not the wheel," countered Autumn Evening, who then turned to the rest of us. "She has no idea how to control the speed. It's kind of exhilarating. You could die at any minute."

"Why don't we walk?" our counselor suggested, mildly insulted, as she popped a fresh Pep-O-Mint Lifesaver into her mouth. She could make those suckers last for hours and I wondered how she resisted biting them.

We issued a group whine and Maddy left to find us a boat driver. My bunkmates and I sat by the Boys' Side dock, waiting, when suddenly a vision appeared. He was tall and handsome with curly blond hair, a sixteen-year-old god with a learner's permit. He was Aaron Klafter. He was a new camper. He was from exotic Cheyenne, Wyoming.

"Says he can drive the boat," Maddy informed us. "We'll see."

Aaron looked at us, shyly, and then at last he spoke: "Hey."

No other words were needed. We climbed aboard. Aaron expertly guided the boat across Lake Wallanatchee, the cold wind whipping through his curly locks. When we arrived at the Girls' Side dock and got out, I thought about flashing him my best smile, but realized it wouldn't mean much with all the metal in my mouth. With his help, I gracefully stepped out of the boat. Then, once on my own, I tripped.

Back at the bunk, we got ready for bed, even though this camp didn't seem to have any notion of a curfew. We would have stayed up all night talking about Aaron, but Maddy went to sleep early. She'd done this all three nights so far, which struck me as odd. Wasn't the whole point of being a counselor for the evenings off? For hanging out with the rest of the staff and doing things you couldn't do when you were thirteen? I wondered if Maddy was unpopular and had no social life. Was that going to happen to me?

"Hey!"

It was around two in the morning.

"Hey, Mindy!"

Someone was shining a flashlight in my face.

"We're going on a raid," Autumn Evening whispered. "We're going back to Boys' Side."

I jumped out of bed. A raid! I'd always wanted to go on a raid and here I was.

Betty was muttering something in her sleep and Hallie wasn't interested in going, so it was just me, Dana, and Autumn Evening. We crossed the lake by canoe and soon discovered why this was not encouraged. Even with the moonlight shining down on Lake Wallanatchee we couldn't see the rocks. There were many. In the fifteen minutes it took us to cross we nearly capsized four times.

"Anyone in particular you're interested in?" I dared to ask as we paddled, crashed, and paddled some more.

"Not really," said Dana, but I could tell there was someone.

"I just like looking at them when they're asleep," Autumn Evening explained. "Gives me an idea what they'll look like when they're dead."

I looked at Dana. She was looking at Autumn Evening. Autumn Evening was looking at the moon.

Several hours earlier, meeting the boys at the social hall had been an awkward experience. Roaming into their bunk in the middle of the night was entirely different. Illuminated only by our flashlights, the visit was far more casual, much like the way the boys lived. The Foxes' bunk was significantly larger than ours but felt cramped thanks to its state of total disarray. Dirty clothing was piled up and tossed about, mixed in with crushed potato chips and half-eaten Slim Jims still in their wrappers. Even the beds were all out of order, pulled away from the walls and turned at odd angles, not lined up neatly like ours. We'd been at camp for less than a week, but the boys had managed to give their bunk a lived-in look, as if it hadn't been cleaned in at least a decade. And everyone was too tired to care.

Still, I was in the company of two girls who knew how to get a guy and I, their student, tried to remain awake and focused. Autumn Evening made the first move. "I'm cold," she said.

Here is the beauty of being thirteen in 1974: if you were naive enough (and I was) it seemed grown up yet somehow safe to get into bed with a boy you didn't really know. Autumn Evening got an invitation from Chip Fink and crawled in. Kenny Uber untucked his authentic red and black buffalo plaid blanket and motioned to Dana, but she declined.

"I'm going for a walk," she said.

Part of me wanted to go along with her, but more of me wanted to stay right there, wishing and hoping I might be Kenny's second choice.

"Um, I'm really cold, too," I said.

Kenny didn't seem to hear me. He was too busy watching Dana. I said it again. Louder.

"Shoulda brought a jacket," he said, then paused to look at me. "Were you at the social hall tonight?"

"Well, yeah, I—"

"I don't remember you."

"You're teasing, right?" Dana yelled from the doorway, on her way out.

Kenny sighed and pulled a thin rolled-up blanket from the foot of his cot and handed it to me. Not exactly the response I'd hoped for but still not a total rejection. I wrapped the blanket around myself, leaned against the side of his bed, and tried to engage him in conversation. "So how many summers have you been coming here?" Kenny snored and rolled over. I was smitten.

By dawn I was sore and shivering and in need of a bathroom. When I got up and looked, I couldn't find one. Philip Selig was also awake and sitting up in his bed.

"Bull's-eye!" he almost shouted, as he successfully shot a rubber band off his braces, hitting a sleeping bunkmate in the face.

"Is there a bathroom somewhere?" I asked.

"Up in there," he explained in a loud whisper, pointing through a window to a shack on a slight hill. "The toilets, sinks. Everything."

"Everyone shares?" I asked. "All of Boys' Side? That's gross."

"Think of it as historical," Philip said, crawling out from under his old wool blankets and reaching for his Mets cap. "Think of it as tradition. Back in the early days here they didn't have that much plumbing."

"Think of how disgusting it must be in there," I said.

"Yeah, it is pretty bad," he admitted. "Especially the toe jam in the showers."

"What's a toe jam?"

Philip grinned as we stood in the doorway. "You're such a girl."

I left the Foxes' bunk and walked over to the shower house and up to the door. It smelled like a cesspool, which was not surprising since that was the camp's plumbing system. I shouted hello. Someone called back. I ran.

I thought about running through the light drizzle all the way back down the dirt road, along the highway, then down the Girls' Side road and back to my bunk. After only twenty feet, I ran into my counselor.

"Uhhh . . . what are you doing here?" I asked.

Maddy looked at me and squinted. "What are *you* doing here?" she countered.

"Um . . . I asked you first."

Incredibly, she accepted that. "I go to bed early every night," she said, "so I can get up early and jog."

Maddy would run to Boys' Side then meet up with the food truck and get a ride back. She seemed very devoted to keeping off that weight.

"But Mindy, you're not really supposed to be out of the bunk at this hour," my counselor explained.

"Oh, well," I said. "I'm new here. I don't know the rules."

Maddy nodded.

She figured she might as well stop by the Boys' Headquarters and wake head counselor Jacques Weiss. Classically tall, dark, and handsome, Jacques was one of many foreigners on staff. Saul had long ago discovered he could get deals on airfare and import European counselors who'd then work for free. Most of them were Christian and most would visit the United States just this once; therefore, eight weeks in the backwoods of Maine with a bunch of American Jews formed the basis of their entire impression of our country.

Jacques was unique among the foreigners, and not just because he was Jewish. At thirty-one years old he was still in school, in Paris, working on an elusive PhD. "A professional student," my uncle the high school guidance counselor would call him, Jacques kept his summers free to keep coming back to Kin-A-Hurra.

"Wanna wait for me and ride back on the truck?" Maddy asked.

"I would, but . . ." I was growing uncomfortable, so I took a deep breath. "Did you know there's just this one disgusting bathroom for all of Boys' Side?"

Maddy got the hint.

As it turned out, Boys' Headquarters had its own private stall and she led me in. She was still inside, in the back room with

Jacques, when I came out again so I took a seat on the porch and waited. He must have been a heavy sleeper. I waited for at least twenty minutes.

"Good morning," I said to Jacques, when the two finally appeared.

"Mais oui," he replied, with a sly grin.

Jacques let me ring the bell to wake up Boys' Side. A few minutes later, Autumn Evening strolled over from the Foxes' bunk and Dana emerged, alone, from the Giant Teepee at the far end of the softball field, over by the flagpole.

On the ride back, amid a truckload of waffles, we learned that Dana had met up in the night with Aaron Klafter.

"We went into the teepee to look at the stars," she told us.

"Really? You can see through the top?" I asked. "It looks all closed up."

Dana paused. "Nothing happened, okay?" she insisted.

It didn't matter to me. All that mattered was that she wasn't interested in Kenny and that I had one less obstacle to deal with in this, the summer I was going to get a boyfriend. And not just *a* boyfriend, *the* boyfriend. The one I wanted. The one I had to have.

It was Kenny Uber or bust.

"There were five, five constipated men
In the Bible, in the Bible
There were five, five constipated men
In the Five Books of Moses
The first, first constipated man
Was Cain, he wasn't Abel . . ."

3

MY MOTHER'S MOTHER, GUSSIE BARUCH, DROPPED OUT OF SCHOOL at the end of sixth grade and went to work in a factory. There, her older, worldlier coworkers introduced her to Chinese food—the official nosh of the assimilated Jew—and it was the beginning of the end of keeping kosher. Within a few years, Gussie met my grandfather, Max Leventhal. Max's mother did not approve of the undereducated factory girl; she attempted to break them up by first moving the Leventhals from Brooklyn to the Bronx, then drinking a bottle of iodine in protest. The iodine did not kill her, nor did it deter young romance. Max and Gussie were married in 1924.

Gussie promised her new mother-in-law that she would keep a kosher home and she did. But on Sundays, while my grandfather read the paper, she told him that she was taking their two daughters (my mother and my aunt) "downtown to see the relatives." This was code for "I am taking them out of the house to eat nonkosher Chinese food." My grandfather would smile, say, "Send the family my regards," and turn the page.

Gussie had it easy. After my parents married in 1957, there would be no more visits to the relatives downtown. My father was the son of eastern European immigrants, a man who would have fit right in at a seventeenth-century shtetl, adamant about sticking to the Old World dietary laws. This meant we kept two separate sets of dishes in the house, one for dairy foods and one for meat. We did not eat meat and milk together. We did not eat pork or shellfish. Ever.

These rules were difficult to explain to my friends, particularly the matter of vegetable shortening versus lard. I couldn't eat Hostess cupcakes, but Drake's were okay. I couldn't have Oreos, but I could gorge on Hydrox. Pepperoni pizza at birthday parties posed multiple layers of nightmares, as did sampling the food we made in Home Ec class. To this day, I'm not sure if I'm supposed to eat Jell-O.

Camp Kin-A-Hurra was on the list of acceptable summer camps because, in our kitchen that winter evening, Saul Rattner smiled widely and assured my father, "We are strictly kosher!"

If only my father had known the truth.

Although the camp did own two separate sets of dishes, the Girls' Side kitchen staff found the bone china designated for meat too hard to clean. They decided to go with the plastic dairy set full-time and I decided not to tell my father.

Of course, I felt bad about the deception. Jewish guilt is a very real thing. I grew up with a lot of pride in my heritage, wanting to embrace it, to celebrate its history. But the way my father insisted we observe every minor holiday we couldn't even pronounce and stick to every obscure rule ("No ripping toilet paper on Saturdays!") made it tedious and time-consuming and I came to resent it. Which made me feel guilty. It was with this familiar feeling of trepidation that I approached the first Friday night at camp. Sundown marks the beginning of *Shabbos,* the Sabbath.

Up until the 1960s, summer camps operated like small private countries with official camp uniforms in official colors. Most of this went out the window by the end of the cultural revolution and, by the mid-seventies, Kin-A-Hurra had developed its own unofficial daily uniform. If you were cool, you wore a T-shirt (really cool if it featured the Coca-Cola logo in Hebrew) and denim painter's pants or overalls. To complete the outfit, you wore a red or blue bandanna tied to the hammer loop on the thigh. Luckily, I had plenty of painter's pants. They were not a big seller in Springfield, New Jersey, and had been on sale in every color at Rynette's. On Friday nights, when we were expected to wear white to welcome the Sabbath, I pulled on and zipped up my white discount painter's pants.

Boys' Side and Girls' Side held separate services on Friday nights. Ours were in my favorite building, the Point, and the waitresses dressed it up for the occasion, draping bedsheets over the tables to simulate tablecloths. By each place setting sat an over-ripe piece of cantaloupe and a Xeroxed booklet containing the evening's prayers. Because there was no rabbi, head counselor Wendy Katz was in charge. She asked us to turn to page one. Then she asked us to stand and then be seated. And then we turned to page twelve. The service was short and sweet and to the point. Best of all, there was no sermon.

We concluded the service by singing the blessing over the candles, which were already lit, and the blessing over the wine, which was really grape bug juice. And then came the blessing over the bread. Based on my Kin-A-Hurra experience so far, my expectations were nil when this first sliver was handed to me, which made it all the more spectacular when I bit in. On Friday nights it is a Jewish tradition to eat challah, braided egg bread, and this was the real thing, made fresh by Walter Henderson, the chef across the lake who'd been employed by the New York State prison system for more than thirty years. After three decades of serving up bread and water, he'd certainly mastered the bread part. It was soft and sweet, manna from Boys' Side that would arrive once a week and nothing like the loaf my mother picked up each Friday at ShopRite.

After the dishes were cleared away, old mimeographed songbooks were passed out. It was nice to have the faded purple ink words in front of us, but most of us already knew these songs, some of which were in Hebrew and others in English. Though the camper population was quite diverse, coming from twenty-three states and five foreign countries (apparently Saul duped Jewish families 'round the globe), our religion, our shared ancestry, bound us together. Well, that and the fact that we were all stranded in this dump for the summer. I mouthed the words silently, so as not to ruin things, and enjoyed the concert.

The next morning, Saturday, services would be co-ed and held over on Boys' Side. I expected this to be my next chance to see Kenny—but, to my delight, he showed up in our bunk that night, at three a.m.

The creaky screen door woke me as he entered.

"Kenny?"

I thought I was dreaming.

"Hi," he grunted, peering around in the dim light. "Which bed is Dana's?"

"Dana? Why would you want to see her?"

"Never mind. I found her."

Kenny kicked the foot of her bed, "accidentally" waking her up.

"Oh, hi," she yawned in his face.

"Nice pajamas," he whispered.

"Shut up," Dana laughed as she sat up, pulled out her ponytail holder, and fluffed her hair. "Hey," she suggested in a sudden burst of genius, "wanna walk me back to Boys' Side so I can go see Aaron?"

"Aaron?" Kenny gulped.

"Yeah, c'mon, it'll be nice. We'll walk around the lake."

Kenny was looking at the floor. "I guess," he said quietly.

"Hey, I'm awake, too," I whispered.

They turned to me.

"You want to come with us?" Dana asked.

"Sure!"

I grabbed some clothes and raced to the bathroom to throw them on, unable to make out the muffled exchange between Dana and Kenny. When I returned a minute later, the three of us slipped out of the bunk.

Except for the fact that he was standing next to the woman he loved, I had Kenny all to myself.

He turned to Dana. "You know, if Aaron's asleep—"

"Of course he'll be asleep," I interrupted. "It's the middle of the night."

"If Aaron's asleep," Kenny continued, ignoring me, "you can hang out with me, *Dana*."

"Oh, thanks," she said. "But I don't think he'd mind if I woke him up."

This wasn't going the way I'd planned. Kenny was acting like he was interested in Dana even though he knew she liked Aaron. Perhaps he thought he could still win her over, but not if I won him over first.

"I'm not busy," I offered.

Kenny hesitated, which I determined had to do with the temperature. Even though it was early July, the night air was cold and we shivered as we walked down the dirt road and around the lake. Kenny put his arm through Dana's and picked up the pace. I tried to keep up, found I couldn't, but failed to see the metaphor.

I arrived at Boys' Side ten steps behind them. Dana thanked Kenny, then said good night to us and headed off. It was just the two of us now, the moment I'd waited for, the reason I was here. My chance to flirt. If only I knew how.

"So what do you want to do now?" he asked.

I wanted to cross my arms and blink my eyes and make him like me. Instead, I just shrugged.

"Do you sing on Boys' Side?"

"What?"

"Sing. At services. On Girls' Side, after dinner, everybody sings. It sounds really pretty. I don't really sing, but . . . What songs do you like? What are your favorite prayers?"

"I don't know," Kenny muttered, then stuck his hands in his pockets and looked around.

I needed to regain his attention, to make this sound interesting.

"I like 'Dona Dona,'" I offered. "Well, I like how it sounds with the harmony and the melody. Do the boys sing it with the harmony and the melody? Actually, if you think about it, it's pretty sad. I mean, it's a whole song about a calf about to be killed. I wonder why we sing that."

"Uh, I don't know . . ."

"I kind of like 'Zum Gali Gali,' too," I went on, waving my hands and gesturing, as if this made my story more exciting to hear. "There's this one girl, Erica, she's only eight. She's from Queens. She likes to stand on the table and lead us in it. I also like 'Hava Nagila,' especially when you change the words to 'Have a banana,' even though I don't really like bananas. The smell bothers me. So far Friday night is my favorite part of camp. How about you?"

I'd thought about if for months, what I'd say or do when I was alone with a boy I liked and now, here I was, talking about songs and bananas.

Kenny looked at me like I'd just stepped off a spaceship.

"I think my counselor might be looking for me," he said. "I think I have to go back to my bunk. Uh—see you at services, I guess."

Kenny turned and walked away, but I clung to his last remark. It was surely an invitation. I'd see him again in a few hours.

For now, I needed to get back to my bunk, too. Unfortunately, I wasn't that familiar with the layout of Boys' Side since I'd seen it only in the dark. I knew where the dock was, behind the dining hall, and I walked down to the beach where I found a canoe with a paddle in it. I pushed off and climbed in and, since I didn't have a life jacket, prayed I wouldn't tip the boat over or fall out, as I once again hadn't passed my deepwater test.

There was a reason why I was a terrible swimmer. It was all because of my nose. At my former camp and at the Springfield Community Pool, girls were required to wear bathing caps. But if you are a girl with a prominent proboscis, you do not want to put one on. No number of floppy plastic flowers adorning your headgear can detract from the fact that, without your hair to hide behind, you are nothing but a giant nose. I hated swimming because I hated bathing caps because I hated my nose. And because of this, I was sure, my crush on Kenny Uber was going to end up with me drowning.

I paddled slowly at first, feeling for rocks and straining to see if I was heading in the right direction. And then I heard it—*Vrroooom!* My concentration was broken by a sudden, thundering noise. The motorboat!

"Hey, lookit! Think I see someone!"

"Where?"

They were men's voices, yelling, and they were heading my way. It flashed across my mind that it might be Jacques Weiss or Saul Rattner, coming to get me for being out of my bunk in the middle of the night. Saul would throw me out of camp and send me home to my parents and my parents would be furious. Even if they let me out of the house, I'd end up spending the rest of the summer at the Springfield Pool with my bathing cap on my head, watching my little brothers, while fat women in muumuus and shower caps hogged the shallow section when they announced it was time for the Ladies' Daily Dunk.

I ducked down so no one would see me as my canoe rocked from side to side in the wake created by their boat.

I wondered if Kenny would miss me if I left. I hoped so.

"Nah. Don't see nobody," I heard the second man shout as the motorboat zipped away. Close call, but I was undetected. They didn't sound like Saul or Jacques and I didn't care who they were as long as I wasn't in trouble. I made it back to Girls' Side in what seemed like both an eternity and a matter of seconds, jumped out of the canoe, pulled it ashore, and ran back to my bunk. I tiptoed quietly up the creaky front steps, slipped in through the creaky porch door, and slid into my creaky metal army cot.

Betty sat up and looked at me.

"Going to be late for swim instruction," she said.

"But it's the middle of the night . . ."

Betty not only talked in her sleep, she also got up and did things. In this case, she went over to her cubbyhole, pulled out a bathing suit, and put it on over her clothes. Then she got back into bed and pulled the covers over her head. She was in for a surprise when she woke up the next morning. Meanwhile, a heavy rain began to fall, wiping out all other sounds, and I drifted off as well.

At breakfast a few hours later, the girls from the oldest bunk, the junior counselors who lived up the hill, were not in attendance and no one knew why. It crossed my mind that they might have heard about my adventure and now they were off at some secret meeting, some chic restaurant where sixteen-year-olds go, drinking black coffee, smoking Virginia Slims, and laughing behind my back.

"Did you hear about Mindy?"

"Went to Boys' Side last night."

"To see Kenny. What a dope!"
"As if some boy would like her."
"As if Kenny would like her!"
"Can I bum another smoke?"
Was it narcissistic to think people were talking about how unimportant I was?

After breakfast, it was time to go to Boys' Side for services, which now seemed like the last thing I wanted to do. Walking around the lake midmorning was not the same experience as walking there at night. As we paraded by, the sunburned townies at the Public Beach glared at us, inadvertently calling up the opening scenes from *Deliverance*. And then there were the bees. One of the cottages was owned by a beekeeper and during the day his little pets were out in full force. A swarm had descended upon the dirt road just a few feet ahead and we stood there, eighty-five of us, frozen. "Just walk slowly," the man in the head-to-toe protective beekeeper's uniform told us. "They're really friendly."

I'd had encounters with bees before. At Camp Cicada I'd managed to accidentally step on a hive while on an overnight in the woods when I was hunting for a marshmallow stick. I figured the eight stings were due punishment, since my plan was to rip a live branch from a tree in order to toast calories I didn't really need. My counselor said it was no big deal and I should cover the stings with mud. By the next day my whole leg had swelled up. Now, on the road to Boys' Side, I was facing hundreds, maybe thousands, a solid wall of bees.

"What's the matter?" Dana asked.

"I think I might be allergic," I explained.

"Just walk really fast. And close your mouth," Dana advised. "You don't want to swallow any."

She had no idea I had the potential to swell, to look like a hippo or an elephant or one of those balloons from the Macy's parade. And that certainly wasn't going to impress any boys.

The old-timers, experienced with this routine from summers past, led the way. They walked ahead, albeit stiffly and carefully, then motioned to the rest of us. Most of the newcomers tentatively followed, walking a little bit faster, almost running, trying not to scream, as that would have necessitated opening their mouths. Even the youngest girls got up their nerve. I couldn't be the only chicken. I clenched my fists, held my breath, and walked as fast as I could through the bees until I joined the rest of the group. Sure enough, the man in the full-body protection was right—no one got stung. Once we were all well past the bees, we ran. This unpleasant ritual would be repeated weekly for the entire summer.

We arrived at Boys' Side about fifteen minutes early. Kenny came bounding up to me.

"Hi," he said. "How are you?"

I was nearly speechless. I couldn't believe he was talking to me. *Maybe he'd come to his senses overnight?*

He asked, "You get back okay last night?"

Kenny was all but ignoring Dana, who was standing next to me. It was too good to be true. I had to say something. Something clever. Something that had nothing to do with singing or how bananas smelled.

"Um . . . yeah. I got back okay."

Something better than that, but someone was heading toward us. It was Philip.

"Mindy! Hi!"

It was the worst possible moment. Couldn't he tell that I was talking to Kenny because I wanted to be talking to Kenny and I didn't want to be talking to him?

Evidently not.

"Wanna see something cool over in the Social Hall?" Philip asked, then, finally noting my expression, "Oh, did I interrupt?"

"Well . . ." I began, turning toward Kenny.

Kenny was busy watching Dana talking to Aaron.

Philip had messed up everything. And what was worse, it was possible Kenny still liked Dana, even after the way she'd snubbed him the night before. Unless, I thought, *It's bothering him that I'm talking to Philip because it's bad for me to be talking to someone most people ignore and, as Kenny's girlfriend, what I do reflects on him.*

It was all very complicated.

But talking to someone no one else talks to shouldn't make me look bad. It should make me look . . . kind. And everyone likes kind people.

So I decided to ask Kenny if he'd mind my leaving with Philip, but Kenny was gone.

Philip led me into the Social Hall and behind the darkened stage. I had no idea what he wanted to show me and wished I had a set of keys with me so I could do that thing where you place them between your fingers, just in case.

But instead of lunging at me Philip pointed up to the rafters. "Look. See?"

Campers' names and their years of attendance were painted everywhere. At first sight this was nothing special. It is a summer camp tradition to sign your name, to leave your mark so people will know you were here, old-fashioned legible graffiti. I could tell you exactly who had lived in my bunk in 1966 and every summer since. It's also a tradition that when the walls get too full, they are painted over to make room for the next batch of names.

Backstage, however, the walls had never been repainted. These were the names of campers from the early days, including the dead ones Autumn Evening Schwartz claimed to be in touch with. Philip showed me his favorite autograph: *Harold Selig '22–'30.* "That was my grandfather," Philip explained. "My father's father. He was one of the first campers when he was a kid." I tried to imagine my own father's father, Sam Schneider, as a child, but couldn't see anything other than the bald-headed eighty-year-old with the phlegmy cough and stubbly beard cheeks that felt like I was kissing a hairbrush.

"There was this group of Zionists," Philip explained, thankfully breaking my reflections on Grandpa. "You know, those people who promoted the idea of the state of Israel? Saul's great-uncle was one of them. They started this camp."

"So it's been in his family for, like, fifty years?"

"Uh-huh."

"Wow. The only thing that's been in my family for fifty years is the good silverware, which we never use because, you know . . . it's good."

"I think we have the same set at our house," Philip said. He smiled and I could see his teeth were pretty white under all that metal. "And don't tell anyone, but the blankets on my bed? They're like thirty years old. Belonged to my dad when he went to camp here."

Philip and I had way too much in common.

"So how many kids were here the first summer?" I asked. "How did they know how many bunks to build?"

"They got twenty-five boys from New York City to come up here on a train and pitch tents by the lake. There weren't any bunks."

"No bunks?" I was stunned. "But I'll bet Saul's great-uncle lied and told all the parents they had them."

"Probably," Philip laughed. "'Oh, Harold, you'll love it in Maine! We have heating and plumbing and Scott Joplin teaches piano and we'll show you how to Charleston and . . . and . . .'"

"'And there's not a single mosquito!'"

"That's right," Philip said. "'Oh, and there's girls!'"

"Wait. There weren't any girls?"

"Not for the first few years. The girls came later."

"Are you sure?"

"Yeah. I wrote an essay about camp for school."

"About this camp? They let you do that?"

"Not just Kin-A-Hurra," Philip explained. "About the history of all camps. Back to before there were any."

Before? I knew there was radio before TV and straight-leg jeans before bell-bottoms, but a time without camp? I'd never considered this.

"In the early days," Philip told me, "boys would go out in groups with a leader who taught them how to pitch tents and cook over a campfire, their rugged lives emulating Civil War heroes."

"Emulating," I said. "You copied that out of *The World Book*, right?"

"You want to know about this stuff or not?" he asked.

I may not have been interested in the Laura Ingalls spinning wheels and butter churns my parents dragged me to see, but I did want to know more about these pioneers.

Philip continued, explaining how, over the next hundred years, what was once the domain of small groups of farm boys with high aspirations and a love of the land devolved into masses of suburban Jews with name tags in their underpants heading into the woods to write letters home complaining about it. I wanted to ask Philip more about the history of this particular camp, but Jacques rang the bell, summoning us to services.

Rows of weathered, dark red benches faced a large tree by the edge of the lake. This was our holy place. The tree was unique, actually two trees growing from one trunk, side by side. A big wooden box was firmly nestled between the two halves. This box was the *Ark* and it contained the camp *Torah*, the parchment scroll from which scripture was read.

Saul (who claimed to have graduated from some obscure rabbinical college but then chose not to be ordained) stood at a podium in front of the Torah Tree and officiated. Wendy Katz, head of Girls' Side, had no power here and became just another person in the crowd. She took a seat on a front row bench. Kenny was seated with his bunkmates, so I headed for a spot a couple of rows away. Philip sat down next to me, but when I thought Kenny was looking I got up and moved, even though I knew it was a mean thing to do.

I wouldn't have had this choice to make at home. In the old days in Europe, when my ancestors had lived like the characters in *Fiddler on the Roof*, Orthodox Jews expected the women to sit in the back or up in a balcony, the way some people in the southern part of this country were once expected to ride at the rear of the bus. But by the time our crowd crossed the Atlantic, most Jews had already discovered that with assimilation came options.

"Reform is lazy; Conservative is hazy; Orthodox is crazy." That's how my friends at my Conservative Hebrew School kept the three kinds straight.

"It's never a good thing to be more religious than your religious leader," my mother noted one Yom Kippur, as we walked to temple and the rabbi drove by, waving. "Merry Christmas," my mother shouted, waving back.

My father was thrilled when an Orthodox congregation from Newark relocated to Springfield and he expected the rest of our family to be excited about it. I wasn't crazy about converting to Crazy, sitting with my mother on the other side of a curtain. I felt like an imposter on *To Tell the Truth*, surrounded by real Jews straight out of old photos from Poland, only with better hats. Despite my confused and negative feelings, I wanted to remain attached to my religion. The Jewish people are the perennial underdogs, like lefties or substitute teachers, and I felt it was important for us to stick together.

I had no idea that most of my fellow campers were Reform and not the least bit observant at home. Sure, they knew the words to the songs we sang on Friday nights, but they never thought twice about eating a quarter pounder and a chocolate shake. For most of them, this was exposure to something new and only for me was it a relaxation of the rules.

Saul's sermon was a little bit different from what I was used to at home, the blaming and finger pointing and accusations of sins I could never even think of committing.

"Are you listening, Mindy?" my father would lean over and ask.

"Uh-huh," I'd lie, then immediately realize this was a violation of at least one of the Ten Commandments.

Saul's speech this morning, however, was riveting. Instead of preaching, he used the time to explain that the oldest group of girls, the junior counselors who were now in attendance, had spent the night at his house after intruders threw rocks at their bunks and called to them to come outside. "The prowlers," as they henceforth would be known, had come by motorboat, launched from the Public Beach.

"That's who I heard last night!" I whispered too loudly to no one.

"Shhh! We want to hear what he's saying," Betty snapped at me.

"The girls' screams scared them off," Saul explained, "but we'll take a few precautionary measures. No need to alarm your parents, though. No need to mention it in letters home. You're all safe."

Saul had the perfect plan for keeping Girls' Side secure. Until the prowlers were caught, there would be no more walking around or canoeing across the lake at night alone. If you needed to go on a raid, you had to wake a counselor to drive you.

Jacques jumped up and shouted out an even better plan.

"What if we have ze oldest boys, ze junior counselors, sleeping in ze girls' bunks? For to protect them?" Everyone liked Jacques's idea (as well as his Pepé le Pew accent), especially the sixteen-year-old boys. Since this was the 1970s, when no one knew any better, it was approved. Until the prowlers were caught, junior counselor Aaron Klafter would be living with us, camped out on our front porch. Services had ended with Dana's prayers answered. Mine would have to wait a little longer.

In my father's Orthodox congregation, watching the other worshipers, I could never grasp their connection with God. But on Friday nights at the Point and on Saturday mornings at the Torah Tree by the lake, I felt something else. "Lazy-Hazy" Camp Kin-A-Hurra's version of religion worked for me. And until the prowlers were caught, there was only one day a week when I could be certain to see Kenny Uber. For the first time in my life, I started looking forward to Saturday morning services. Which made me feel guilty.

to the calypso tune
"Man Smart, Woman Smarter"

"We came to camp
We thought it was co-ed
But after a day
This idea was dead
A line was drawn
Across the camp
And over this line
We dare not tramp
Ah so, Camp Director he say
That the boy and the girl must be kept away
But oh no, to Uncle Saul's dismay
Biology always finds a way"

4

THERE HAD TO BE A WAY TO MAKE KENNY NOTICE ME, TO MAKE HIM like me, to make him like me more than he liked Dana, but this would not be easy to do. On Sunday morning it was announced that my bunk and the next oldest, the fourteen-year-olds, would have auditions for *The Sound of Music*. There was no way I dared compete with Dana for the role of Maria von Trapp.

It's not that I had trouble getting up onstage in front of a crowd. In fact, I had long dreamed of a life as a performer. In my younger days, I'd wanted to be a ballerina, until first grade when I took lessons and my dreams were shattered. It was not the glamorous life I had anticipated, the one I imagined the little plastic girl spinning around in my jewelry box led.

Classes were held at three p.m. in my school gymnasium and we changed our clothes in the girls' bathroom with its gritty sinks and tile floors that reeked of excess Comet. Judy Horowitz's hand-me-down leotard and tights were too small for me and it hurt to stand up straight, which is not helpful in dance. What's more, I was an absolute klutz. Ballet was not my calling and I was devastated. At the age of seven, I had no idea what to do with the rest of my life.

There are no guidance counselors at the elementary level, and for months I wandered the halls of the Raymond Chisholm School in silent anguish. The summer brought little relief as I struggled in vain to improve my crawl stroke at the Springfield Community Pool. I practiced in the shallow end where the old ladies in shower caps dangled their toes over the edge and never actually got in. They shouted at me to stop splashing them. My vacation was no vacation as I found myself flailing and failing at everything I attempted.

Then, in second grade, Miss Rispoli awarded me the lead in our class play, *The Cross Princess,* because I had the loudest voice. Not exactly one of the classics, *The Cross Princess* took up nine pages in my advanced reading group's textbook and could be performed in about fifteen minutes. As Princess Annabelle, who refused to get enough sleep and was therefore cranky, I had the second-most lines in the play after Gregory Fitzgerald, five inches shorter than I, who played the king and somehow had more to say. I wore my favorite dress-up outfit, the gigantic pink taffeta ball gown my mother had saved from the 1950s and would later give away to the cleaning woman without first asking me. I was loud; I was clear; I was the Cross Princess. I knew then that I was going to be an actress. Still haunted by the ballet fiasco, I kept the plan to myself but was relieved to once again have a long-term goal.

For the next couple of years my life picked up. I'd even overcome my klutziness to some degree when I went off to day camp the summer after second grade. Drama counselor Winston Kemp wrote and produced an original play about a circus tiger adapting to life on a farm and I excelled in the role of a dancing ear of corn. My father hadn't been able to take time off from work and my mother hadn't yet learned how to drive, rendering them unable to attend the performance. Determined they would share in my exultation, and in spite of the fact that it had started to rain in the middle of the play, causing my green and yellow crepe paper costume to dissolve,

I wore the remains home on the bus and reenacted the dance for my entire family in the middle of the kitchen while my mother prepared lamb chops, Minute Rice, and wax beans.

But soon, oh too soon, my luck ran out. It happened during my first summer at sleepaway camp. Every play put on at Camp Cicada was an adaptation of an extravagant Broadway musical, though they kept the costs down by doing only the first act. Due to this restriction, the two oldest bunks' production of 1776 ended with Congress still in disagreement and nobody ever signed the Declaration of Independence.

When it came time for my bunk's play, I wasn't sure if I could sing well enough. Though everyone in my family loved to sing, I suspected we were not worthy of acclaim. One time, while walking around the block with my mother and learning the words to "Jeepers Creepers," a kid passing by on a red tricycle rang the bell on the handlebars with the streamers and asked us to "quit disturbing the peace." The King Family Singers had nothing to fear from us.

Further decreasing my chances for a plum role in the play was the fact that I was unpopular at Camp Cicada and feared I might not get cast at all. I opted to go for the biggest nonsinging part, which was also a nonspeaking part, and played Nana the dog in Act I of *Peter Pan*. It gave me plenty of time onstage, even if I couldn't show off my loud voice, and best of all it was a role no one else wanted.

My chance to sing anonymously would arise later in the summer during "The Annual Girls' Side Sing," a competition in which a theme was chosen, the counselors wrote songs, and the campers performed them. There were no individual parts to play so we would all be treated as equals. Supposedly. This year's theme was

"Women's Rights" and my counselor, Sherry Merlin, wanted to win. We rehearsed for three days straight and were even excused from General Swim. Hours before the performance, which would be judged by the Camp Cicada boys, we ran through the songs one last time. In the middle of "Susan B. Anthony / You have done so much for me," Sherry stopped us.

"I think someone is slightly off-key," she remarked. No one responded.

Anxious to win my bunkmates' favor, I raised my hand. "I guess it might be me."

Sherry thought for a moment, then looked at me sternly and said, "You know, sometimes *not* singing is just as important as singing."

I nodded in agreement. What else could I do? That night, as I stood onstage, I mouthed the words. When we came in second, I knew it wasn't my fault we'd lost, but being asked not to sing in public had a lasting effect and I vowed never to do it again.

The one exception was my bat mitzvah. Because the Orthodox synagogue didn't offer a Hebrew school, my parents maintained a membership at the town's Conservative temple, in spite of the fact that my father considered it slumming. My parents enrolled my brothers and me at Temple Beth Shalom where the principal, Mr. Lazar, was forever warning us that our Hebrew school grades would go on our permanent records. These thrice-weekly sessions were so excruciatingly boring that one day I brought along a Tootsie Pop and really did count how many licks it takes to reach the chewy center. Eight hundred and sixty-four. I also made sure to make the Honor Roll every semester and upon graduation received a certificate with a shiny gold sticker, which I promptly stuffed in a drawer in my bedroom.

Orthodox girls don't have to become bat mitzvahs but, thanks to my family's dual citizenship, mine had taken place a few months before coming to Kin-A-Hurra, shortly after I turned thirteen. I wasn't thrilled about singing solo, but luckily a bat mitzvah isn't like a Broadway show. The range of musical notes is limited as are the audience's expectations. The rabbi was kind enough to tape-record the event and hand me the cassettes afterward. To this day I have not had the nerve to listen to myself, but I must have done all right since the invited guests handed me envelopes with checks at the luncheon following the service.

So far no one at Kin-A-Hurra had heard me sing and I intended to keep it that way. "The sound of music" was not likely to be the result of anything emerging from me. I thought about not auditioning at all, but Kenny was planning on being in the play and I couldn't risk losing a chance to be around him. It was time to go to Boys' Side and try out for a new role.

There were too many of us to fit into the Valiant. Because we were the camp without a school bus, we climbed aboard its substitute, the Green Truck. Built in the dustbowl of the 1930s and intended for moving cattle, the Green Truck had open, slatted sides and a rickety metal roof. I'd seen it for the first time when a load of boys showed up to "borrow" our softball field to stage an egg fight, then left without cleaning up. Dana caught me staring in disbelief as the truck's back gates swung open and people piled out, and she leaned over and whispered in my ear, "We think Saul bought it on sale after the Holocaust."

Once inside, I learned that the truck possessed a hard wooden floor and no shock absorbers, so the slightest bump in the road could send you flying. All the Dramamine in the world wouldn't have been enough for my brother Jay to last a fifty-foot journey.

The rear gates had a tendency to come unlocked and swing open in the middle of traffic, so Maddy and the other bunk's counselor stood at the back and held them shut.

Fourteen-year-old Mindy Plotke leaned over to me and said, "Can you believe this thing? The Joad family wouldn't be caught dead in this." I smiled and nodded and pretended to understand the literary reference, though it would be another three years before I'd be assigned to read *The Grapes of Wrath*. Saul had warned me there would be a "cartload of Mindys" at camp, but pretty, petite Mindy Plotke and I were currently the only ones. Since she was a returning camper and I was new, she was known as Mindy and I was Other Mindy.

Kin-A-Hurra theater director Rhonda Shafter was a former Broadway star who'd made quite a splash in a show called *Fresh Faces of 1929*. Her deep, bellowing voice had kept her out of Hollywood's new talking pictures, but she sang and danced for many years on the Great White Way and now found it her duty to nurture the next generation of stars. Rhonda was more than sixty years old and more than sixty pounds overweight. In spite of this and her three-pack-a-day Lucky Strikes habit, she danced with grace and, clad in one of her signature caftans, huffed and puffed as she tried to explain the difference between upstage and downstage and why "stage right" meant left.

Surprisingly, Dana was not a shoo-in for the lead. With the fourteen-year-olds auditioning as well, there were several girls who could pull off "Do-Re-Mi." Dana, who took private voice lessons in Manhattan, narrowly did capture the role and I wasn't entirely jealous. As the daughter of an Orthodox Jew, I wasn't sure how my father would feel about me cavorting on stage in a nun's habit. The role of Liesl, the beautiful girl who sings "Sixteen Going on Seventeen" was the one I secretly coveted. I fantasized all the time about being a beautiful sixteen-year-old. That was the age at which my parents had promised I could get a nose job.

There were a couple of decent-sized nonsinging female roles and I read for the part of the elegant but disliked Baroness. As soon as I spoke my first line, Rhonda yelled, "Stop!" and went into a coughing fit. But what at first appeared to be her standard round of hacking turned out to be a moment of elation.

"Everyone, listen," she said. "Do you hear how loud this girl is?"

Terrific. Now I was too loud.

"This is how I want you all to sound."

I was stunned. Rhonda asked me to turn my script to the page with "Do-Re-Mi" while motioning to the Kin-A-Hurra waiter-turned-accompanist to play the piano. This was it. My big chance. If I could sing, Rhonda could replace Dana with me. And if I could replace Dana in the play, then maybe I could replace her once and for all in Kenny's heart.

I got as far as warbling the first line of the song, and then I remembered Sherry Merlin's words: *"Sometimes not singing is just as important as singing,"* and I stopped.

"Is there a problem?" Rhonda asked.

A problem? Was she kidding? If Sherry Merlin was right and I couldn't sing, then everyone else was about to find out. Worse, if it turned out that I could sing and I won the part away from Dana, then Dana wouldn't like me and then everyone else would hate me.

I answered Rhonda's question. "I don't think I can do this."

Rhonda was very disappointed. I would not be her newest discovery. I told her I would feel more comfortable with a non-singing part, but instead of being cast as the glamorous Baroness I got the role of Frau Schmidt, the frumpy old battle-ax housekeeper.

"How come you gave up?" Autumn Evening asked me later. "You sounded okay on that first line. Maybe not for Maria, but you could've had some other singing part. You could've had mine."

I wanted a lot of things Autumn Evening had. Cast as Liesl, she would be performing "Sixteen Going on Seventeen" with Kenny as Rolf, the misguided Austrian youth. And not only would she get to sing with Kenny, she was well on her way to achieving her long-term goal of becoming a famous writer. During the winter, Autumn Evening's piano teacher had helped her complete a musical comedy about the philosophy of pure reason, *You Kant Take It With You*, for which casting would begin in early August. Encouraged by her family, she was always coming up with interesting ideas and finding ways to make them come to life. She was a totally free spirit and no one ever stepped on her spontaneity and joy.

While most Jewish children are named in memory of a deceased relative as a means of keeping that person's spirit alive, Autumn Evening's parents wished for her to be an original. They named her after a season filled with awe-inspiring color and a time of day associated with calm. I was named after two great-aunts who were killed by the Nazis. In Yiddish, my name means "Sea of Bitterness."

After getting over my initial envy, I was happy she'd gotten the part. Autumn Evening was not looking for a boyfriend, and if I couldn't play opposite Kenny she was a safe second choice.

Fourteen-year-old Borscha Belyavsky was a recent emigrant from the Soviet Union whose new synagogue in Canarsie, Brooklyn, had paid her camp tuition and sent her to Maine in an attempt to hasten her Americanization. This might have worked out if she hadn't already decided for herself what being American meant. She'd seen enough of our finest prime-time TV to know what to do. Modeling herself after J.J. from *Good Times*, she shouted out "Dy-no-mite!" when cast in the role of Mother Superior. I was curious to hear "Climb Ev'ry Mountain" sung with a strong Russian accent. Mindy Plotke and my bunkmate Hallie Susser would be the other singing nuns.

We had exactly one week to prepare and, like a trained summer stock company, we focused all of our energy and attention on the play. With the exception of meals, sleeping, and running to Boys' HQ to use the bathroom, we spent all of our time in the Social Hall. My bunkmates and I brought along cards and jacks and taught the boys how to play since their chosen indoor activity, floor hockey, was deemed too noisy and disruptive during rehearsals. I tried to get close to Kenny, complimenting him on his voice and how well it blended with Autumn Evening's soprano. "She's okay," he said, "but I wish Dana was playing Liesl."

"Can you believe it?" I commented to Autumn Evening one night on the truck ride back to Girls' Side. "He doesn't get it. He keeps on chasing after someone who just isn't interested."

"It's the story of the ages," my bunkmate assured me.

After a few days of being rebuffed, Kenny gave up and found an excuse to get out of the Social Hall, volunteering to go down to the Arts & Crafts shack to help make the flats for the scenery. During a lengthy choreography session for "So Long, Farewell," during which my part was to stand off to the side and nod my head as each child exited, I sneaked out and went down to see if I could help, too. The Arts & Crafts shack was full of girls, several of them fawning over Kenny, but that wasn't going to get in my way. Philip Selig was going to get in my way. He was the only other boy there, and when he saw me come in he practically lunged across the table to strike up a conversation.

"Had any good schnitzel with noodles lately?" he asked.

"Not exactly one of *my* favorite things," I replied.

The sad truth was, I found Philip fascinating. He had the best memory of anyone I'd ever met and could recite the entire Gettysburg Address, the American Dental Association's message on the back of the toothpaste tube, and all of the countries in the world in alphabetical order, but I did not want to flirt with him. I wanted to help Kenny pound nails.

Before volunteering my skills, I noticed that the two boys were doing the carpentry and the girls were doing the artwork. This was so typical. On Girls' Side we were forever stringing beads and making sand candles while the boys got to do the good stuff. Here on Boys' Side, they made Centauri model rockets and shot them off in the middle of the softball field, next to the Giant Teepee. Because the field was surrounded by woods on three sides and by the lake on the fourth, once a rocket was launched its designer was unlikely to get it back. Eventually, they realized that building rockets was a waste of time and switched to gluing used Popsicle sticks to the engines, not caring what happened after takeoff.

"Got any more green?" I asked. Afraid to flaunt my strength and coordination once again in front of Kenny, I grabbed a brush and joined in painting pictures of shrubbery, while ignoring Philip and gazing at the object of my so-far-unrequited love.

Dana lost her voice the day before the performance, which caused Rhonda Shafter to smoke a fourth pack of Luckies and pull me aside and ask, "Darling, do you know Dana's lines? The words to the songs?"

I did. I could recite everyone's lines from the play as well as several choice scenes from *The Mary Tyler Moore Show*, the entire *Haftorah* portion from my bat mitzvah, and, like Philip, the verbiage from the back of a tube of toothpaste.

"If she doesn't get her voice back, you're the singing nun."

"Really?" I questioned her. "Would it be that big a deal if we just waited until tomorrow night or the next night or whenever she got it back? I mean, that only seems fair."

"Kiddo," she told me, "show biz ain't about what's fair."

It was like something out of an old black-and-white movie or a miracle from the Bible—or at least it might have been if it had come to pass.

After spending the entire day resting and drinking tea with lemon (which Kenny was only too happy to fetch), Dana got her voice back an hour before the show. It was time to get into our costumes. Once out of her nun's habit, Dana would get to wear a fabulous blue dress that tied in the back and showed off the fact that, unlike mine, her body went in at the waist and out at the chest. I got to wear a size eighteen maid's uniform, which someone on the Boys' Side kitchen staff had borrowed from a relative who worked in a retirement home. Maddy did my hair for me, pulling it back in a bun to look more maid-like, but it only made me look the way I did at the Springfield pool in my bathing-capped all-nose days.

Philip, in charge of opening and closing the curtain, told me I looked cute so I stuck my tongue out at him. The play was well received and no one seemed to mind that the seven von Trapp children were all approximately the same age as each other and everyone else in the show. Dana, of course, got a standing ovation.

At my former camp, there was a counselor, Lorelei Cohen, who was studying to be a professional choir conductor and, after plays, she would lead us in the Camp Cicada anthem, the words to which were shown on an overhead projector. The song contained many phrases I found repugnant and I was relieved to be only mouthing the words "Happiness has found us/Pure love surrounds us/Cicada, I pledge to thee." After that, we'd crowd out the door, pushing and shoving for no good reason other than that was what we did. I expected pretty much the same thing here, but Camp Kin-A-Hurra had no official theme song. Instead, we sang "Taps":

"Day is done / Gone the sun
From the lakes, from the hills, from the sky
All is well / Safely rest
God is nigh"

Because there was no overhead projector, a lot of people sang it wrong and the last line came out "God is nice." A pleasant thought, but I was a stickler for accuracy and let this error bother me all summer.

We were the second group to put on a play this season and I wondered if the same thing would happen after "Taps" that had happened the week before, following the nine-year-olds' production of *The Me Nobody Knows*. Sure enough, everyone in the audience ran up onstage and congratulated everyone in the play. Even me. People I barely knew were hugging me and telling me I was great and they sounded like they meant it. This went on for about ten minutes, and when the crowd onstage finally cleared, Philip headed toward me, arms outstretched, so I waved, jumped down, and looked around for Kenny.

I found him. He was watching something in the shadows at the back of the stage and he had a sad, hurt look on his face. Kenny was watching Dana and Aaron, partially hidden behind the stage curtain, locked in an embrace and a long, lingering kiss. Their secret was out. Now everyone would know they were a couple. Even Kenny. Dana was no longer available for the role of girlfriend.

And I was the understudy, waiting in the wings.

*"Second verse, same as the first
A little bit louder and a little bit worse"*

5

"JUST FIVE MORE MINUTES. PLEEEASE!" EXHAUSTED FROM HER WORK
on the stage, Dana wanted to sleep through breakfast and Maddy,
who lived to avoid confrontation, gave in. The rest of us trudged
down to the Point for reheated eggs while Dana went back to sleep.
Or so we thought.

About twenty minutes later, with her stomach growling, Dana
heard the Food and Garbage Truck rumble by and figured she'd
hitch a ride halfway down to the dining room. Another one of Saul's
bargain purchases, this small blue roofless vehicle, a poor cousin
of the Green Truck, was used to transport meals from the boys'
kitchen to the girls' dining room. Maddy rode it back after her
morning jogs around the lake. The driver, a wild-eyed toothless
local man named George, would deliver the food and then use this
same truck to pick up the big metal garbage barrels around camp
and take them to the dump in the next town.

Evidently George was a gentleman who wouldn't dare enter
one of the girls' bunks to use the bathroom, so while he was taking a whiz against a tree, Dana secretly climbed onto the back of
the truck and hid behind one of the barrels. Her plan to discreetly
hop off at the flagpole was foiled when George didn't stop there—
or anywhere else on Girls' Side—and Dana soon found herself, clad

in red-and-white-striped Dr. Denton feet pajamas, speeding down
the dirt road and heading for the highway.

"Hello! Stop! I'm back here!" Dana yelled, but George couldn't
hear her over Jim Stafford's "Spiders and Snakes," blaring from
the radio as the truck careened onto U.S. Route 2. Hanging on
for dear life, Dana was pelted with spoiled produce, empty Herbal
Essence shampoo bottles, and pages from discarded issues of
the *Weekly Reader*. George finally came to a stop at the Skowhegan dump. When he hopped out and walked around to the
back, he found Dana lying on the floor, filthy and gasping for
breath.

"Look at the mess ya made," was his lone comment. George
had other "errands" to attend to (code for shooting at rats in the
dump) and ordered Dana off the truck.

"But I'm not even wearing any shoes," she complained.

George pointed into the Skowhegan hole.

"Might find some in there."

Forced to walk a mile down the side of the highway, destroying the cozy feet part of her evening wear, Dana found a pay phone
at a Flying A gas station. Not having any change with her, she called
the camp's Main Office (one of the dilapidated cottages adjacent
to Saul's grand house) collect.

"So sorry," the woman from Yorkshire, England, who'd been
hoodwinked into working in the office all summer replied. "We
mustn't accept collect calls."

Dana's first three attempts failed. On her fourth try, she said,
"This is Dana Bleckman's mother" and the call went through. Fifteen minutes later, Aaron picked her up in the Valiant and drove
her down to the Point.

Their entrance prompted a Dedication. The Dedication is a
means of mass communication across a dining hall, what smoke
signals were to the Indians, what semaphore was to the navy, what

the Internet is to nerds. Upon sighting the new couple, everyone spontaneously paddled their hands on the tables, then shouted in unison, "Quiet, please, dedicated to Dana Bleckman," and then began to sing to the tune of "My Darling Clementine":

> *"Dana Bleckman, Dana Bleckman*
> *Take some good advice from me.*
> *Don't let Aaron, Aaron Klafter*
> *Get an inch above your knee.*
>
> *He will tell you that he loves you*
> *And he'll fill your heart with joy.*
> *Then he'll leave you broken-hearted*
> *With a bouncing baby boy."*

Dana tried to blush, but I suspect she was pleased to be serenaded. Aaron was embarrassed for real and left (and later, at Maddy's suggestion, packed up and moved back to Boys' Side, though he was still welcome to visit on a regular basis).

Meanwhile, the attention focused on Dana didn't end there. She was next called upon to sing one of her songs from the play and did a reprise of "My Favorite Things." Autumn Evening, Borscha Belyavsky, and eventually everyone who'd sung the night before got a chance to belt out tunes in front of the Point's big stone fireplace. This had happened a week earlier with the cast of *The Me Nobody Knows* and, before that, girls who'd sung in shows in previous summers were also put on the spot. At Kin-A-Hurra, accomplishments were celebrated over and over again, year after year. Only Betty Gilbert (who'd somehow landed the role of the Baroness) and I were left out.

Just as things were winding down, head counselor Wendy Katz announced that we'd been invited to a day of intercamp games with Camp Morningside, an all-girls facility in the nearby town of Waterville. The mention of Camp Morningside brought snickers from the old-timers. I imagined there was some deep-seated rivalry. Wendy came over to my bunk's table and asked if any of us played softball.

Why did it have to be softball? I was panic-stricken, but not in the way I was about singing. I wasn't afraid I wouldn't be good enough; far worse—I was probably too good. This had been my downfall back home. I had once been fairly popular among my classmates in Springfield, but things had changed recently, especially regarding the boys. New Jersey was the first state to recognize Title IX, the ruling that allowed girls to play in the boys' baseball leagues. I wasn't the very best player in girls' softball, but I was among the top few and assumed my peers would all make the switch over to baseball. As it turned out, I was the only one, an accidental trailblazer.

There was a rule in the baseball league that every kid on the team had to play a minimum of one inning on the field and have one turn at bat. And that was all I ever got—the minimum. With barely any playing time, I never had a chance to excel, but it did change my status from Smart Likable Girl with an Unfortunate Nose to what felt like Official Town Pariah. I didn't want the same thing to happen here. I kept my hand down.

"Mindy, don't you play some sport or something?" Autumn Evening called out.

"Kind of."

"Softball?" Wendy half asked, half begged.

I didn't want the boys to know I was a jock. I didn't want Kenny to know I was a jock. But Morningside was a girls' camp. I figured I was safe.

"Well. Yeah."

"Great! You'll be the captain. Thanks for volunteering."

"Captain. Cool." Autumn Evening patted me on the back.

"If you need any extra gloves," Wendy added, "we can borrow them from the boys."

"Because they won't be there, right?" I asked with confidence.

"Of course not," she said. "They'll be busy playing with Morningwood. That's the boys' camp next door. They're playing basketball, I think."

And we'd all be riding there together in the Green Truck.

Softball suited me for a couple of reasons. My father had grown up playing baseball in vacant lots in Jersey City and, though my brothers inherited his passion for the sport, I was the one who inherited his ability. Unlike faster-paced sports, a softball game plays out like a drama, capable of unfolding slowly and taking many twists and turns. A team certain to lose can always make an amazing comeback and triumph in the end. Yogi Berra was right: "It ain't over till it's over," a sentiment I hoped applied to more than just ball games. And while there is room for individual glory in a game, it's unusual for any one person to be totally blamed for a loss. I like a sport where you don't get blamed.

After retrieving our bats from the junior counselors' bunks (where they were keeping them for protection from the prowlers), I assembled a team that was not expected to win. My goal was to have everyone know which hand to wear the glove on so we might not be completely humiliated. The fourteen- and fifteen-year-old girls would be playing volleyball against Morningside, just as they had the year before, but I was informed there was no rivalry between the two camps. "We always lose," Mindy Plotke told me. "That's why we're always invited back."

Out on the open road, aboard the Green Truck, most of the girls stood by the sides, sticking their heads through the slats and mooing at passing motorists. Our manly counterparts, however, sat hunched together in the center, with Kenny leading a discussion of their team's strategy. Not too many top players in the NBA are Jewish, but it isn't for lack of interest in the sport. While the goals for the summer varied by age group on Girls' Side, every boy in camp shared one common interest: to do nothing but play basketball. On rainy days, while we were inside shuffling cards, reading comics, and endlessly blow-drying our hair, the boys were outside in their bathing suits, dribbling and shooting in and around the puddles.

"Kenny, you really think we can win?" Chip Fink asked.

"This'll be the biggest slaughter of all time," his captain assured him. "Like—like—"

"Like in the '68–'69 season when the Knicks beat the Pistons 135–87?" Philip offered.

"Sure," Kenny said, sharing a high-five with Chip. "Just like Mr. Peabody over here says."

As our truck lurched through Morningside/Morningwood's fancy wrought-iron gates, the mooing ceased as the Kin-A-Hurra girls burst into song. To the tune of "Auld Lang Syne," they announced:

> *"We're here because we're here because we're here*
> *because we're here / We're here because we're here*
> *because we're here because we're here."*

I, meanwhile, was astounded by the camp's Tara-like splendor. Manicured lawns, neatly planted rows of trees, even the sun was out. It looked like . . . the camp in the photos Saul had shown us in our kitchen!

But there was something wrong with this perfect picture. The girls were all dressed identically in stiff blue cotton uniforms that snapped down the side, like something from a bad parochial school gym class, and the boys were in what resembled prison-issue shirts and shorts. Now I knew why our older girls dressed the way they had. That morning, the doomed volleyball players spent much time pairing up striped shirts, polka-dot shorts, and argyle socks in an effort to create the most garish outfits possible. Following that, they painted freckles on their faces and braided their hair over wire hangers, pulling it out to the sides, Pippi Longstocking–style. Facing imminent defeat, they mocked their opponents' dress code, choosing to score points for cleverness if not returns over the net. There was something else I noticed: none of the Morningside/Morningwood campers looked happy. I wouldn't have imagined it was possible, but this place appealed to me even less than pristine, perfect Camp Cicada.

The outlook wasn't brilliant for the Kin-A-Hurra Nine this day. The gum-snapping captain of the Morningside team greeted us by saying, "We're gonna kill ya," to which I replied, "I'm sure you will." And while it is customary for the visiting team to bat first, the bossy girls of Morningside insisted on being up so we took the field.

"Sue, Sue, she's our man—if she can't do it, Margaret can!"

Morningside cheered in an attempt to psych us out, but mostly we commented on how there weren't any good gender-specific girls' cheers and maybe we should write some on the way home in the truck.

I took my place on the pitcher's mound as Morningside's Sue took a few practice swings. On a real team, the kind where you have a chance in hell, I am a first baseman, but today I had to pitch since I was the only one who could lob the ball anywhere near the plate. The first pitch I threw was a strike. And then two more. Sue, no doubt as shocked as I was, didn't move her bat and struck out. My teammates cheered me as the Morningside girls razzed their player and she slunk back to the bench to hang her head in shame.

The second Morningside batter, the menacing Margaret, spat on her hands and then rubbed them together, glaring at me as she tightened her grip on the bat. I threw another perfectly good pitch and she hit it straight at Dana who was playing second base. In a defensive move meant to preserve her teeth and singing voice, Dana stuck her glove in front of her face. The ball landed in it and stayed there. Second out. Our team went wild and suddenly a remarkable transformation began to take place: we started to care. The third batter tapped the ball back to me and I jogged it over to the bag for the last out. Based on the squeals of delight emanating from my teammates, you'd have thought we'd won the whole game, not just the right to bat.

Several members of my team made contact with the ball, one even got to first base. We didn't score any runs, but the mere fact that the game remained tied 0–0 after the first inning was nothing short of miraculous. I've always resented teams that huddle and pray before a game, as if they assume God has time for amateur athletics and that, if He did, He'd care who won. But today, you had to admit, God was on our side. The Morningside girls were thrown by our lucky breaks and it affected their game. They bobbled the ball in the field and criticized each other while we continually congratulated one another just for trying. By the middle of the fourth inning, we were down by only a run with one more turn at bat.

And then the umpire called "Lunch!" In the middle of the game. I thought it was very polite that they were offering to feed us, but as it turned out that wasn't the plan. Like everyone else at this camp, the kitchen staff at Morningside kept a very tight schedule and we had to interrupt our game for the host team to go eat. The kids from Kin-A-Hurra were expected to wait outside on the field.

"You know," observed Dana, "I think we could actually win this game. How weird would that be? I never win anything."

"You never win?" I asked, stunned.

"I wish I could play softball like you," she said.

"Yeah, me too," added Autumn Evening, who had obviously not played ball in any former life.

"Yeah, well, what do you think they're eating in there?" I asked. "Caviar and steak tartare?"

"Or maybe the bodies of the last camp they played," Dana offered.

Which might have been tastier than what we were having for lunch.

This was a Thursday and on Thursdays the Kin-A-Hurra kitchen staff had a break from the end of breakfast until it was time to prepare dinner. For them, it was the closest thing to a day off. For the rest of us it was Sandwich Day, which meant dried-out peanut butter and runny jelly slapped onto white bread about to sprout penicillin. To wash it down, there were industrial-size cans of peach nectar and for dessert there'd be grapes. Bushels and bushels of grapes. Saul must've known someone in the grape business. We made the sandwiches every week, but we never ate them. When it came time for lunch we'd head for O'Boyle's, a lonely little general store, conveniently located across the highway from us. Luckily, I'd been saving up money all year: dimes from my grandmother when I visited her on Sundays, the eight dollars I got from my aunt and uncle for Hanukkah, most of my thirty-five-cent weekly allowance, and the two dollars my mother paid me one time for helping her weed a flower bed. O'Boyle's ended up with the bulk of my fortune, but today we were stranded in Waterville and most of us simply chose to go hungry.

"You're still here?"

That was the greeting we got from one of our opponents when they returned to the field after lunch.

"We were hoping you'd leave."

Not only had we stuck around, the older Kin-A-Hurra girls and all of the boys, having finished their games, arrived to watch us. Including Kenny.

"Bet we massacred you little faggots," one of the Morningside girls called out.

"What're you talking about?" Kenny yelled back. "We whipped your asses!"

It was true. While the Kin-A-Hurra volleyball team had triumphed in wardrobe only, all of that practice in the rain paid off for the boys and the Kin-A-Hurra team beat Morningwood handily. Now the Morningside girls were playing for honor and revenge.

Hannah Moss, our catcher, was only seven years old and short for her age. She could barely hold up the bat.

I pulled her aside and asked, "Can you stand like this?" and demonstrated crouching down so that my knees were in my armpits as I held the bat over my head. "The strike zone is between your knees and your armpits."

"But if I stand like that," she said, "there is no strike zone."

"Exactly."

Hannah was a very smart seven-year-old who giggled as she crouched by the side of home plate. Four pitches in a row sailed over her head, the umpire called them balls, and she walked to first base.

"Other Mindy, she's our man—if she can't do it . . . we're gonna lose!"

My teammates' hopes rested with me, like Casey of Mudville. If I could hit a home run, we would win. I watched the first pitch come toward me. It looked pretty good. I thought about swinging and then I had another thought: *Kenny is watching. If I hit a home run, he'll know the truth about me, that I'm probably a better athlete than he is.* It was like that moment at the end of *Annie Get Your Gun* when Ms. Oakley had to decide whether or not to best her beau, Frank Butler, in a shooting match. But I didn't know what decision she'd made. When I saw the play at Camp Cicada, it ended before they got to that part.

"C'mon! You can do it! Other Mindy! Other Mindy!"

The shouts weren't deafening but, all in all, pretty loud. I didn't swing. Strike one.

"Time!" Autumn Evening brought the game to a halt, jumping up off the bench and running over to me.

I stepped out of the batter's box to see what she wanted. "What is it?" I asked. "You don't even know anything about softball."

"I saw this old movie once," she explained. "There was a guy who pointed to the outfield and then hit the ball there. He looked like Oliver Hardy. Only without the mustache."

"I think you mean Babe Ruth," I told her. "He played for the Yankees."

"He's a real guy?"

"He was. He's dead now."

"Would you like me to get in touch with him?"

"Um, maybe later. We're in the middle of a game. Is there something you want to tell me?"

"Yeah. Hit the ball like Babe Ruth. I know you're kind of shy, so you don't have to point first. Just hit it really far so we can win this silly thing and you can be the hero. Or heroine. No, that sounds like drugs. Be the hero. I mean, unless you're afraid or something."

"Afraid?"

"Well, you're not one to jump into the spotlight. You're always hanging back, like you're thinking about doing something, but then you don't. What are you so afraid of?"

What was I so afraid of? I was afraid of screwing up, of letting people down. That's why I couldn't tell my parents how upset I was when we pulled into camp that first day. If I'd told them I was disappointed, then they'd have been disappointed too, like the time I showed my father an A I got on a book report and he said, "How come not an A+?" Grades were really important in my family. We were all supposed to be geniuses even though only Jay was really that smart. Still, we were expected to get A's all the time, except in penmanship, because that didn't reflect how smart you were and also because both of my parents had really bad handwriting, to the point where no one could read our grocery list so we always wound up buying the wrong stuff at the market, and somehow I'd get blamed for that, too.

It was as if, no matter how hard I tried, nothing I did was ever good enough. And if nothing I did was ever good enough, then maybe it was best not to try. Maybe it was best just to stand around and watch other people do things, watch other people live. What was I so afraid of? I was afraid of everything, which is why, sometimes, it was easiest to do nothing.

"Earth to Mindy," Autumn Evening broke in. "Are you even listening? Lookit, this isn't like singing—which by the way you're fine at—or straightening your hair. You can do this."

I knew she was right. And I wanted to be popular and I wanted to save the day, but was this the way? Was it worth winning a dumb old softball game if I risked losing Kenny before I'd even gotten him? As the first girl to play baseball in Springfield, New Jersey, I'd found out what it was like to have kids and their parents swear at me and accuse me of destroying the Great American Game. I was certain I would never have a boyfriend at home. Camp was my only chance.

As I stepped back into the batter's box, I glanced over at the crowd from Kin-A-Hurra. Everyone was cheering me on. Everyone. I realized I couldn't let them down. I couldn't let myself down. If I was going to get a boyfriend this summer, it was going to be because of who I really was, a lefty who could hit the ball to right field, the position where the other team always puts the weakest player.

The next pitch was good and I turned my body toward first base as I swung, delivering a strong line drive. It went over the infielders' heads and onto the grass where, like the girls from my hometown softball league, the right fielder watched it go through her legs. When I crossed home plate, the victory was ours. The Kin-A-Hurra contingent raced onto the field where Hannah and I nearly had our eyes gouged out by the wired braids of a dozen shrieking Pippi Longstockings.

On the truck ride home, we stopped at a place suspiciously named Dairy Kween and Kenny came over to me and told me how wonderful I was.

"You're amazing," he said. I thought this might be the best day of my life until he added, "You should've been a guy!"

Another boy felt differently. He pushed Kenny out of the way, proclaiming, "I'm glad you're not."

"Mindy Schneider, Mindy Schneider, take some good advice from me . . ." shouted one of the older girls.

And with that my fate was sealed. I was being sung about in public. There was no stopping it now. I had my first boyfriend. Philip Selig.

Just what I was afraid of.

to the tune of
"Pomp and Circumstance"

"Greasy french fries, unscrambled eggs
Soggy toast and sour milk
Walking turkey legs
Shredded cardboard and Ill-Bran
Fish that never swam
Vinegar and STP
Peanut putty and jam
Live, watery bug juice
Hot dogs that bark
Hamburgers made of Alpo
Jell-O that shines in the dark
Doughnuts used for anchors
Olympic shot-put pancakes
These are the meals they serve us
Just like mother makes"

6

I HAD SO COMPLETELY DEVOTED MY LIFE TO TRYING IN VAIN TO GET A boyfriend and then dealing with defeat that it never crossed my mind what I'd do if I did actually get one. Especially if it was the wrong one.

I'd been successfully ignoring and avoiding Philip for days, choosing to remain on Girls' Side, hiding out in other bunks. I improved my jacks game, learning three new fancies, while being tutored on the intricacies of numbing one's eyebrows with an ice cube before tweezing. Life was temporarily edifying and effortless and it made me wonder if there were any kosher all-girls camps, and, if so, perhaps it would be best if I signed up for one the next summer. My self-imposed exile from Boys' Side ended on a Friday morning, when chef Walter Henderson invited my bunk to help him make the challah for that evening. This was a rare honor, not to be passed up.

My bunkmates, counselor, and I rode across the lake on the Ferry, a large Huck Finn–esque motorized raft the camp maintenance man had built on a lark, to see if it really would float. The feeling that came over me whenever I arrived at Boys' Side was that this was the real camp, and that Girls' Side was just some aberration tacked onto the other end of the lake. Girls' Side was hilly, with its randomly numbered bunks secluded among trees, and seemingly empty since we tended to stay indoors. Boys' Side was flat and wide open and its bunks, displaying carved plaques with their picturesque names, were lined up in rows. And there was always activity going on, no matter how hard it rained. Saul Rattner rarely visited the girls. Seeing him on our side was like seeing Sammy Davis Jr. on *All in the Family*. You expected the words "Special Guest Star" to flash in front of him. Big social events were held on Boys' Side. Co-ed Saturday morning services were held on Boys' Side. Saul and his wife ate only on Boys' Side. Even though Boys' Side was a pigsty.

The Boys' Side dining hall was nothing like the Point. While our building was beautiful, cozy, and surprisingly well maintained, the boys' dining hall was a massive aging wreck. While the girls dined at clean, varnished tables set upon gleaming wood floors, the boys sat at old picnic tables on an uneven, beat-up, rotting floor, painted gray with spatters of red, blue, and yellow, as if the primary colors might hide the termite damage and filth. The tables were long and narrow and crowded together and, strangest of all, the boys didn't seem to care.

The youngest bunk, the Pioneers, prided themselves on being assigned the most heavily sloped corner of the room. Their counselor, Bobby Gurvitz, had shown them a neat trick: if you held a saltshaker at the high end of the table and let go, you could send it all the way down to the other end without pushing it. This game became known as "Pass the Salt," but it worked just as well with other condiments, hard-boiled eggs, and a small lightweight camper named Teddy Marcus.

The kitchen wasn't in much better shape. I'd learned in my seventh-grade Humanities class all about the early American peddlers, men who traveled by covered wagon across the prairies, selling their household wares. Walter's pots and pans looked like they'd come from a frontier settler's homestead yard sale. In some ways this was quaint. You knew these old kettles had seen a lot of good home cooking, if not here then somewhere else. The long, wide preparation tables had their charm as well. Girls' Side had only one small aluminum table, but Walter worked on a thick maple base. The wood gave you the feeling that it was homey and sturdy, if not also filled with bacteria festering since the turn of the century. The only perfectly spotless thing in the kitchen was Walter himself. A round-bellied sixty-five-year-old black man from Panama, Walter was dressed in a crisp white chef's uniform topped off with a favorite old fishing hat. This was the man who made the world's best Jewish bread.

"Hurry along there boys, before that nasty cereal sticks to my bowls," Walter warned the waiters. The kitchen staff was running late, still cleaning up from breakfast. It wasn't their fault. They were working short-handed; a waiter had been fired just the night before when he was caught urinating into a pitcher of bug juice he was planning to serve to Saul.

Walter saw us come in.

"I don't understand you kids. I make you nice, hot eggs for breakfast and all you want is Frosted Flakes."

"The eggs are hot when he makes them?" I whispered.

Maddy nudged me. Walter didn't hear.

"Come in, come on in, girls," Walter urged us. "Welcome to my beautiful kitchen."

Walter Henderson had spent thirty-plus years cooking for maximum-security prisoners in upstate New York. Now he was retired and cooking in paradise. We watched as he assembled the ingredients on the long wooden table: vast amounts of eggs, sugar, flour, water, yeast, margarine, and honey. I'd never thought about what went into a challah, just that it came out of a plastic bag.

"You care to join us, young lady?" Walter asked Betty, who was standing in a corner, clutching her current reading material,

Sheila Levine Is Dead and Living in New York, and working hard to maintain her appearance of hating camp.

"I'm busy," she said, but from the way she was peering over the top of her book, I knew she wanted to be included.

"Suit yourself," Walter continued, "but before we start, who knows why we make the challah?"

For all the years of Hebrew school among us, no one knew the answer.

"Maybe *you* do?" I proposed.

Walter let out a sigh. "You kids should know this. Making challah is a mitzvah. Who knows what 'mitzvah' means?"

I knew that one. "It's a good deed."

"Yes. And who knows about the twelve tribes of Israel?"

Hallie took a shot. "Um, there were these tribes. Twelve of them. In Israel . . ."

"Walter, why don't you tell us?" Maddy suggested.

"All-righty then. Eleven of the twelve tribes were farmers, raising their own food. But the twelfth tribe, the Levis, took care of the temple."

"Far out," said Autumn Evening, "and then they invented pants."

"In appreciation," Walter continued, "the other tribes would bring them donations of bread. Challah is the name for the act of separating the piece of bread given to the Levis. It's why we break off a piece when we make the blessing on Friday night and pass it around the table. Sharing is a mitzvah. God's commandment that we make challah is His way of reminding us to share."

"Walter!" Dana shouted out. "We wouldn't care if it was pagan food of the devil. It's the best thing you make. Now show us how!"

Under the master chef's guidance, we mixed and poured and stirred for half an hour. Well, all of us except Betty.

I suspected Betty's aloofness was really a defense, a desire to avoid being ridiculed. I didn't know what she was afraid of specifically, but it was a feeling with which I was well acquainted and the reason I had skipped Arlene Stein's bat mitzvah party a month earlier. Instead of the usual clunky dancing to a fake rock band at some catering hall, Arlene's parents rented out the pool at the YWHA. Picturing myself in a bathing suit in front of thirteen-year-old boys and thirteen-year-old girls, I declined the invitation, opting to stay home and polish off a Sara Lee cake left over from my mother's Cultural Affairs Committee meeting.

After the ingredients were mixed and folded, Walter said we were ready to knead the dough.

"So Mindy, you gonna go see Philip while we're here?" Dana asked.

"He's not my boyfriend," I insisted.

"Ooh, look how hard she's denying it," chided Hallie. "That's a sure sign. So Dana, you gonna go see Aaron?"

Dana smiled. "Um… duh!"

As the boy talk escalated, my bunkmates and I got a little carried away, pounding and punching the malleable bread into submission.

"That's enough, girls! That's enough!" Walter shouted, stopping us before we destroyed it. Next, the dough was placed into a warm oven to double in size. This would take an hour and a half. Time to kill.

I knew Kenny would be playing basketball and Philip would not be, so I ran oh-so-casually as fast as I could to the court, plunking myself down on the sidelines.

"Hi! Whatcha doin' here?" Philip asked.

He was standing right next to me. I hadn't anticipated this scenario. Like water trapped in a hot pot, I could feel my insides about to boil. I was mad at Philip, convinced in my own mind that he'd gone around after the softball game telling people he was my boyfriend. It would make me appear unavailable for Kenny, which meant Kenny would never realize I was interested in him, which meant I would only dream about him more.

"Just came out to watch the game," I said, blasé.

"Kinda dull," he informed me. "Wanna go do something else?"

"Can't. My bunk's helping Walter bake tonight's challah. Well, he's letting us pretend to be helping. It's pretty cool. But I have to stay around the dining hall."

"Ever been upstairs? I could show you."

"Upstairs? Above the dining hall?"

"Uh-huh."

This was one place I was really curious about. I'd heard stories how those rooms were the worst place on Boys' Side to live.

"It's, like, the most disgusting place," Philip said cheerily.

"Why would I want to see that?"

"Because," he explained, "it'll make your bunk look so much better when you go back."

I tried to hide my interest, but Philip was pulling me by the arm, away from the game. I hoped Kenny didn't see him touching me. Or maybe I hoped he did.

We didn't enter the dining hall from the kitchen side; we went in through the opposite end, via the covered porch, a popular spot for sitting and watching the entire waterfront structure submerge in a heavy downpour.

"It's really nice to watch sunsets from here," Philip said.

"Oh, yeah?" I answered. "Well, maybe if it ever stops raining we'll see one."

Once inside, we climbed up a set of creaky old stairs, the kind with a little closet built underneath that seems so perfect for storing winter clothes until you come back a year later and find them devoured by moths and / or destroyed by nesting rats. At the top of the steps, we heard a strange noise. It sounded vaguely human, like moaning. If I believed in ghosts, I'd have believed I was hearing one then. Someone—or something—was in terrible pain. I pulled back and turned to Philip, then sucked in air, ready to scream. "Shhh!" he said and moved closer. I looked at him like he was nuts. Something terrible was going on in that room.

He motioned for me to be quiet and follow him. Scrawny little Philip was very brave. As we tiptoed onto the landing, we could tell where the noise was coming from. It was a room at the end of the hallway, where a woman was moaning in pain. The door was closed. The moans grew louder.

"Should we call someone for help?" I was really nervous now.

"Sounds like she's doing okay," Philip assured me.

A moment later, the moans climaxed with a shriek and then stopped abruptly. *Is she dead?* I wondered. Would I be blamed some-how and, more important, would this result in being grounded and losing privileges? The door swung open and Julie Printz, the coun-selor who ran the girls' waterfront on sunny days and therefore had plenty of free time, stepped out, looking a little disheveled, but hardly in agony.

Not only was she not in pain, she was kind of glowing. Her expression quickly turned to embarrassment when she saw us. As Julie ran down the creaky stairs, I could hear my mother's voice in my head, *"Tie those laces before you trip and break your teeth."* A few seconds later, the waiter who had played piano for *The Sound of Music* emerged. He didn't look the least bit embarrassed.

"All yours!" he shouted as he ran by the two of us.

"Thanks!" Philip called back, grinning, as he watched the waiter bound down the steps after Julie.

I was utterly confused and then it hit me: *Was this sex? This? This was sex?* What the hell was wrong with people? How could this be? I'd never heard these sounds before and my family slept with all the bedroom doors open. All I'd ever heard was my father snoring and I had three brothers. *How did my parents do it? Why would my parents do it? Would my parents do this? Did my parents do this? This? Sex? God. Yech.*

I decided Philip was not the one to ask. He walked into the newly vacated room. "All ours," he said. I didn't move. "C'mon, don'tcha want to see what's in here?" I did. A lone lightbulb dangled from the ceiling and what was left of the pale green paint on the walls (which we'd find out ten years later was loaded with lead) was peeling in large chunks. This place had all the style and wit of a police interrogation room, but it also had a mirror and a cot and I guess, ultimately, that was all that mattered to Julie and the waiter.

"This was what you wanted to show me?" I asked.

"I guess," came the reply. "Wanna get out of here?"

I did, quickly returning to the hallway.

After peeking into a few more rooms, including the ones the Wolverines were crammed into, Philip and I concluded that the first room was, tragically, the nicest and we dubbed it "The Hanky Panky Suite." We were laughing, but I was nervous, afraid Philip might want me to go back in there with him and close the door like the waiter and Julie.

"I think I have to get back now," I said.

"What time is it?"

"I don't know. I just have a feeling."

"'Kay," Philip said. "I'll go with you."

Which was fine with me as long as it wasn't into that room.

An hour and a half had passed and Philip accompanied me to the kitchen just as Autumn Evening, Betty, and Hallie returned from a film festival in the boys' Social Hall where they were screening old *Three Stooges* shorts (less popular ones from the Joe Besser years), which Saul had acquired from a movie theater that went out of business.

"Mindy with a boyfriend. Never thought I'd see that," Betty commented. "Guess you're not who I thought you were."

Which was possibly the nicest thing anyone ever said about me, so I got defensive. "Shut up, he's not—I mean—"

Philip looked hurt, but I pretended not to notice as Dana walked in with the Adonis, Aaron Klafter, and announced he'd be joining us in bread baking.

"Guys can come?" I asked. "Philip, you want to?"

Feeling guilty as usual, I had to make it up to him for my previous remark.

Philip tried to look nonchalant. "Beats watching basketball, I guess."

As we headed into the kitchen, Aaron took Dana's hand. Philip saw it and turned to me, so I put my hands in my pockets.

Rumor had it that Maddy was off with Jacques, some sort of scheduling crisis she had to help him figure out. For a camp that appeared to have no set schedule, she sure spent a lot of time helping him plan things.

The rest of us watched as Walter rolled the dough into nine long snake-like strands. Then, grasping three strands at a time, he braided them together perfectly. "I wish you could've done my hair like that," I told him. "That would've looked good when I was Frau Schmidt."

Once all the loaves were braided, Walter showed us how to paint the bread with egg wash and sprinkle on poppy seeds. This was all a new experience for me, as I was never really exposed much to baking. My mother barely liked to cook and mostly stuck with broiling things. Her repertoire later expanded when the microwave revolutionized the kitchen and she is the only person I know who makes tuna salad in a Cuisinart, which makes it, let me tell you, very smooth.

Betty had returned to the kitchen only to resume peering at us over the top of her book.

"Could use your help here," I said, trying to sound annoyed.

"Oh, all right," she groaned, putting down the book. "I need a brush."

"You can share mine," I said, and she snatched it away from me.

Betty acted like the whole thing was a chore, but she didn't fool anyone. Mitzvah accomplished.

After the bread was painted and seeded, it was ready to go back into the oven, which meant more free time for my bunkmates and me. Aaron suggested swimming, but for the same reasons I'd skipped Arlene Stein's bat mitzvah party, I did not want to go.

"No, thanks," I said.

"Wanna do something else?" Philip asked.

"Yes, go do something with Philip," Dana urged me. "You'll have fun."

I wanted to say no to him, but it had been interesting exploring upstairs and it was uncomfortable standing around in the kitchen once everyone else left.

"Okay, there is something I want to do," I said. "I want to know what's in that closet under the steps."

Philip smiled. "Cool."

The door was locked, but the wood around it was so rotted it didn't take much for Philip to pry it off. He-man that he was, Philip proudly turned to me and flexed his muscles, but his biceps just sort of flat-lined. We gasped as the door popped open, not so much because we were amazed but because so much dust flew out into our faces. Philip took off his baseball cap and attempted to wave it away.

"This is like my grandparents' store," I said.

"Full of old dusty stuff?"

"Uh-huh. Old cartons, old clothes, an old Singer sewing machine with the foot pedal. Old people . . ."

The closet was deep and piled high with boxes. We opened one and found it was filled with blank, yellowing Camp Kin-A-Hurra official Red Cross swimming cards.

"When I went to day camp they used to give these out at the end of the summer," I said. "I was so dumb I didn't notice they gave me the same Beginner card all four years."

"Not much of a swimmer, huh?" he asked.

I grimaced. "Not really. But I got pretty good with that blue kickboard."

At my old sleepaway camp, I'd finally made it to Advanced Beginner, but I never got to Intermediate, due to a mental block about learning how to dive. Something about my fear of going in nose first. Here at Kin-A-Hurra, where it rained every day, they never made us swim. By now I'd be lucky if I could remember how to dog-paddle.

Philip was the kind of geek who kept a ballpoint pen in his back pocket that leaked and left a little circle of ink on the seat of his pants. He grabbed a card and filled it out for me.

"There," he said as he handed me the card. "You've passed Junior Lifesaving. Congratulations."

"Excellent. I'll put this on my college application."

Even though we were joking around, I was oddly aware that I was pleased to have this old document. It felt like I now owned a piece of camp history. I was new here, but this made me feel somehow connected to the past, a part of something bigger, something I wanted to belong to, not to Philip specifically but to everyone at camp in general. Huddled together on the floor of the closet, we opened a few more boxes and found more old documents.

"It's like a museum," Philip marveled. "The Kin-A-Hurra archives."

There were old application forms and receipts from the days when eight weeks cost $350. And then there was a box marked "Evaluations 1949."

"What is there to evaluate?" I asked. "Everything is broken. You think maybe twenty-five years ago this place was beautiful and organized and they cared about keeping it that way?"

Philip pulled out a sheet and read: "Herbert is very selfish. He insists on being first in the shower every day and grabs for extra desserts at meals."

I glanced at the page. "What kind of evaluations are these?"

Philip read another: "Melvin is a tattletale and must learn to respect others' feelings." And then: "Sidney is a wonderful camper. It's a pleasure being his counselor. He gets along with everyone and doesn't have to be reminded to make his bed with hospital corners."

I figured it out. "The counselors evaluated the campers?"

"These guys would all be in their thirties or forties by now," Philip calculated. "Wonder how they'd feel if they knew their counselors wrote about them. Wonder what our counselors would write about us."

"Philip likes to break into closets and read old papers," I offered.

"I'm not exactly alone here," he said defensively.

"Yeah, I'm guilty, too," I said. "So let's do my bunk: 'Autumn Evening is very creative. She tie-dyed sheets at the Arts & Crafts shack and hung them from the rafters around her bed, turning it into her own private little swinging pad. And she burns a lot of incense and thinks no one knows it's to cover up the smell of cigarettes.'"

"That's so cool!" Philip said. "Can I come over and see it?"

"She had to take it down," I explained with regret. "One of the incense sticks touched one of the sheets and burned a little hole in it and we decided it might be a good idea not to torch another bunk. But it was pretty cool. Now she smokes outside by the cesspool."

Philip wrinkled his nose.

"At least it hides the smell. Oh, and 'Betty Gilbert has all the personality of a head of cabbage.'"

"I've got one," Philip countered, then lowered his voice: 'Kenny Uber is a conceited jerk.'"

"He is not," I shot back. "I can't believe you said that."

"Why?" Philip asked. "Do you still like him?"

He looked at me, stared at me, waiting for an answer even though he already knew it. What a relief when Maddy came walking into the dining hall with that same funny glowing look Julie Printz had worn coming out of the Hanky Panky Suite. My poor counselor. She got her thrills from doing paperwork with the boys' head counselor.

Dana and Aaron showed up a minute later, stopping by to check out the mess in and around the little closet under the steps.

"You two have been busy," Dana noted.

I blushed and tried to explain. "We were just—"

"No need," Aaron stated as Dana looked on approvingly.

"We were looking through stuff, okay?" I insisted.

Aaron peered in. "That door opens? Neat. What are all these papers?"

"Mostly stuff about old campers," I filled him in.

"Any of them dead?" asked Autumn Evening, who'd just entered with the rest of my bunkmates. "No, don't tell me. I'll sense the vibe."

"I can't believe you left me out," Hallie said. "This is, like, my favorite thing."

"Snooping?" Philip asked.

"Not snooping," Hallie insisted. "I'm interested in information. It's like detective work."

"Yeah, well, Encyclopedia Brown, you were off swimming."

"Mindy, next time get me," she said, picking up a few papers.

"How was it, anyway?" I asked.

"The usual," Betty sourly chimed in. "We had to get out when the thunder and lightning started."

Betty was dripping all over the artifacts and I determined it was time to shove them back into their boxes. Philip assisted and, as he gathered up the papers, his hands brushed against mine. A lot.

Upon returning to the kitchen, Walter was already working on the *Shabbos* meal, some sort of stew. I was pretty sure his stews had meat in them and was alarmed to see him throwing large chunks of cheese into the pots.

"That isn't really kosher," I mentioned timidly.

"I don't care," Walter told me. "You kids need the protein," then he mumbled something derogatory about Saul under his breath. I liked Walter.

When the challah came out of the oven, we knew it would be amazing and Walter knew we'd be in a hurry to sample it. He warned us not to eat it hot, saying it was unhealthy, but the only thing that made it unhealthy was how good it tasted, prompting us to eat too much too fast and end up with cramps. Stuffed and sick, but not sorry for what we'd done, our group trooped back out to the dining hall to lie down on the benches and recover.

"Wanna see something really old? From the first year of camp?" Philip leaned over and whispered to me.

"If it's a dead cockroach or something, not really," I said, clutching my stomach in contented pain.

Philip pulled himself up and then reached inside his T-shirt, taking out a silver medallion at the end of a chain. It was shaped like the Star of David.

"They gave these out to all the campers that first summer. All twenty-five kids got 'em."

I sat up and looked closely. The back was stamped *Camp Kin-A-Hurra 1922*. Now this was something. Not counting the other twenty-four, one of a kind. Because I have always been a very materialistic person, a hideous thought went through my mind: *If I marry him some day, maybe he'll let me have this.*

I held it between my fingers and looked at it for a long time, during which Philip and I were face to face, but hardly seeing eye to eye. Although Philip was smart and funny and interesting, and probably the most perfect boy for me, there was one insurmountable problem with him: Philip Selig wasn't Kenny.

I wondered if there might be a way to use him to trade up.

"We're the girls that everybody knows
You can tell us by the color of our clothes
We come from the land where the wine
and whiskey flows
We're the girls from the Salvation Army!"

7

It was an evil plan I was concocting and I wanted to confide in my bunkmate Hallie. It made sense that we'd begun spending a lot of time together. We were two of a kind (the kind whose grand-mothers in Florida used words like "charming and smart" while showing our photographs to other old ladies with cataracts) and we both enjoyed doing the same stupid things.

Within the first few days of our arrival at Kin-A-Hurra, return-ing campers were talking about climbing Mount Katahdin. Located a couple of hours away in Baxter State Park, Katahdin was the north-ern terminus of the Appalachian Trail. Everyone made it sound like it was some rite of passage to climb to the top. Hallie and I could not understand why. Why leave the bunk and ride all that way in the Green Truck just to do something so incredibly hard?

Thanks to heredity and the havoc it played on our bodies, Hallie and I already faced enough obstacles in our lives so we in-vented our own, more manageable mountain to conquer. Down by the flagpole, tucked away behind some overgrown weeds, was the lone Girls' Side archery target. Archery was more hazardous than necessary as Girls' Side wasn't particularly well laid out. There was no safety net behind the target, only a little dirt hill. Just above the hill, opposite Bunk Eight (the one with the good showers), was the basketball court. On sunny days, when one might be inclined to pick up a bow, it was common for campers and counselors alike to be out on the basketball court. Not playing, of course, but lying on beach towels, slathered in baby oil, clutching tin foil reflectors and soaking in the rays. With the ozone layer still believed to be intact, there was no such thing as "too much sun," but bathing beauties did have to worry about being shot through the bikini by the errant arrow of an overzealous camper.

Hallie and I called this little dirt hill Mount Katahdin and were proud of the fact that we could run up and down it twenty times in a row. The real mountain was thirteen feet short of a mile high and we'd heard that some clever person had built a thirteen-foot rock pile on the peak to compensate for the difference. Hallie and I built a thirteen-*inch* rock pile on the crest of our Katahdin and took pictures of each other, with our Kodak Pocket Instamatic cameras, waving from the top. Sometimes we would take a break from running up and down to pick flat rocks from the pile and rub them against our noses, pretending this would somehow remove, or at least reduce, the big bumps we each sported.

Girls' head counselor Wendy Katz adored Hallie and this was yet another situation that made me incredibly jealous, but I couldn't blame her for preferring my compatriot. Hallie was like those products advertised on TV, the "New and Improved" version of me. Sure, she was going through an awkward stage now, but Hallie was confident that one day she'd be beautiful, holding no doubt that she'd eventually grow into her features. When I was with Hallie, we would go into Girls' Headquarters, where Wendy lived in a back room, eat Humpty Dumpty brand potato chips from the blue-and-yellow five-gallon tin barrel Wendy had swiped from the Point, and talk about the future.

"I'd like to be either an actress or a Supreme Court justice," Hallie announced one day. "But I'm not sure where you go to college for that."

"Well," said Wendy, "why not study both? Pick a place that has a drama department *and* a law school."

"Law school?" Hallie looked confused. "You have to go to law school to be a judge?"

Wendy nodded. "Usually."

"So what's the best college that has a law school and a drama school?"

"Probably Yale," Wendy said.

Hallie's eyes lit up. "Great. I'll go there."

I didn't want to come right out and say I wanted to be an actress, too. My turn as Frau Schmidt hadn't exactly wowed anyone and, anyway, I knew it was an impractical choice. But I definitely didn't want to go to law school. If I'd known the word "stultifying" back then, I'd have used it to describe the rare visits to my father's office. Fortunately, I had a backup plan.

"I think I want to do something in television," I said. "I read about this company, AC Nielsen. They rate TV shows. People watch TV and then say if they thought it was good or bad. Do you think that's a job? Professional TV watcher? I'm not sure where you'd go to college for that."

"I think you can watch TV anywhere," Hallie said, and turned the conversation back to herself.

Wendy was the oldest person I'd ever hung out with, even older than my counselor, but as much as I appreciated Hallie getting me into places, sometimes I kind of resented my bunkmate's presence.

Then, one morning, a wonderful thing happened. Hallie woke up with a hideous rash on her rear end. We knew immediately that it was impetigo, as the "tushy plague" had been running rampant among the junior counselors. Although she refused to admit it, Hallie liked to hang out in the JCs' bunks so she could poke around for information and she must have picked up the ailment on one of her missions. While the rest of my bunkmates and I were

content with reading *Betty and Veronica* comics, Hallie preferred
the juicier stuff found in counselors' letters to and from their boyfriends, the handwritten pages filled with angst, detailing troubled
relationships.

We knew where she went looking for these. Though she claimed
to have no knowledge of Emily Herskowitz's heartbreaking split
from her long-distance longtime beau, the jig was up when Hallie
broke out in the telltale ass rash. To prevent her from spreading it
to the rest of our bunk, Hallie was quarantined in the infirmary
and forced to stay in bed watching *Andy Griffith Show* reruns. According to her diary (in which *I* later snooped), it was the high-
light of her summer. With Hallie temporarily out of the way, I could
try to get Wendy to myself, maybe even ask her for dating advice,
but I found I was facing a dilemma.

I had taken to occasionally joining Maddy on her early morning jogs to Boys' Side. On this morning, while waiting on the porch
for Maddy to wake Jacques, I overheard Kenny and his bunkmate
Chip Fink talking on their way to the shower house.

"So y'over her yet?" Chip asked.

"I never liked her. She's a priss," Kenny insisted. "I like the
outdoorsy type, y'know? I mean, as long as she's got big knockers."

There was a girl a year ahead of me in school who'd been trying
for a long time to get a boyfriend, but nobody seemed to want her.
Then, when she finally did get one, lots of other boys became interested. Remembering this while listening to Kenny and Chip, I
figured if having a boyfriend makes you more enticing to other
boys, then being with Philip, or at least looking like I was with
him, might make me appear good enough to make Kenny take a
second look. It was all so simple—unless it was more than mere
coincidence that the girl a year ahead of me in school became

popular right around the time she experienced a sudden growth spurt, her cups ranneth over, and that was why all the boys came a knockin'. In which case I didn't stand a chance.

Boys' Side was a busy place, even this early, with people coming and going. I looked up to see Jim Norbert, the man who'd built the Ferry, strolling down toward the lake, toting a sizable coil of dirty rope over his shoulder. Jim was the quintessential Mainiac, a rugged mountain man, prematurely weathered and cantankerous at the age of thirty-five. Standing six-foot-three with not an ounce of fat on him, he looked like what they had in mind when flannel was invented. I'd seen him on the second day of camp, fixing the broken Girls' Side toilets. When I was informed he was the head of maintenance, I assumed he wasn't much good at his job. I'd since learned his real passion was running weeklong canoe trips. This also held little interest for me until I found out he was Kenny's idol.

"Hi, Jim," I called out and waved.

"Mornin'," he nodded as he readjusted the weighty rope.

Jim was a man of few words, not a big help as I was trying to learn more about him in my attempt to impress Kenny.

I knew that Jim lived in a rusty old trailer by the side of U.S. Route 2. I'd stopped by one time, on my way back from an emergency trip to O'Boyle's when I ran out of Juicy Fruit gum.

"You live here?" I asked, trying to sound surprised, even though I was essentially stalking him.

"C'mawn in," Jim said. "Take a look around."

"Not a lot of stuff in here," I noted.

"Nope. The spartan life. Just m'bed, m'radio, and, of course, the guns."

A regular hillbilly rube, I would have thought, except Jim was also a vegetarian who grew his own food, a supporter of nuclear energy, and an avid reader of both *Newsweek* and *Time*, when he wasn't down at the dump shooting at cans with creepy George.

"What's the rope for?" I asked. "Catching the prowlers?"

Jim shook his head. "Still workin' on that. Boys' Side dock come loose. Gonna tie it back up."

"Hey! Jim!"

It was Kenny, returning from the shower house, calling out to his sensei.

"Mornin'."

"Need a hand with something?"

"Nope. I'm fine."

"I'm going on the Katahdin trip tomorrow," Kenny told him. "I'm leading it."

"Katahdin," Jim reflected. "That's a fine little hike." Jim turned to me. "You going, too?"

I'd never considered climbing Katahdin. Until now. There was a trip leaving the next morning, Kenny Uber was going, and there was one more spot available.

Dana had signed up and then dropped out at the last minute, leaving me another chance to replace her. I wanted to confide in Hallie, to ask for advice on whether or not I should go. But as much as Hallie and I were alike and it was good to hang out together, she was still a snoop, a potential gossip not to be trusted. She might tell anyone and everyone *why* I would be going on this trip.

Afraid someone else might grab it first, I went ahead and took the spot. As much as I'd disliked overnights at Camp Cicada, I did own some cool stuff and was pleased to have another opportunity to use my canteen, poncho, and green sleeping bag with the red flannel lining featuring pictures of elk. My parents had purchased these items a few years before when my older brother Mark joined the Cub Scouts and my parents looked forward to his new avocation.

As it turned out, my brother was not meant for the great outdoors. He preferred spending his free time in the Springfield public library, reading about Greek mythology and the history of politics. I'd inherited his camping stuff and was willing to put it to use for a chance to get away from Philip and nearer to Kenny.

I had most of the clothes I would need for the climb: plenty of T-shirts, thanks to Judy's older brother Victor, and a baseball cap from my father's law office with the firm's name embroidered above the brim: Schneider, Waxgeiser, Moskowitz, Pinsky, Fallick and McCullough. The letters were really small. I even had a pair of work boots my cousin had outgrown, but I did not have the right pants for mountain climbing. Judy Horowitz had worn flimsy elastic waist shorts that would have ripped in a second and my painters' pants were simply too bulky. I needed to borrow something. Bigger than my bunkmates and my newly svelte counselor, I headed up the dirt road that led to the junior counselors' bunks. Secluded in their own little cul-de-sac, these three bunks were known as the Havens, though right now they were just a haven of impetigo.

Hesitant about borrowing things and embarrassed by my size, I timidly entered Haven One where I was assaulted by the commingling scents of Jean Naté After Bath Splash and marijuana. The girls were busy playing backgammon and Chinese checkers and applying cotton balls full of calamine lotion to their backsides, the stuff you did when you couldn't go near the boys, the stuff (I would realize too many years later) that was a lot more fun than what I was doing. Except for the itching.

Stoner Stacie Hofheimer looked over at me. "You toke?"

I'd never even smoked a cigarette.

"Uh . . . what flavor is it?" I asked.

"Acapulco Gold."

The first time I'd seen those words was on a black T-shirt at the mall. I thought it was a vacation resort, the kind of place other families went to while mine went to Pennsylvania to look at Amish people. Stacie handed me the joint and I pretended unconvincingly to know how to hold it. I may as well have been handling a power tool or a pork chop.

"Just suck it in and hold it," she instructed me, as if it was the natural thing to do.

I held on to the joint and stared at it as it burned down closer to my index finger.

"Um, actually, I'm going to Katahdin and, um, I need to borrow some pants. If anybody has a pair . . ."

Stacie took back the joint. "Katahdin, eh?" (She was from Canada.) "Pretty clever plan."

"Why'd you say that?" I asked, panicked she could see through me, right to my heart.

"Just got a boyfriend and now you're going away. Good way to make him miss you. Pretty sneaky."

Stacie had a brand-new pair of Levi's. We wore the same waist size, but she was tall and thin and the pants were five inches too long for me.

"So cuff them," she suggested.

"These are brand-new," I reminded her. "You don't mind? They might get dirty if I'm climbing a mountain."

"That's the whole point. I want you to break them in for me."

I was thrilled. New pants meant Judy Horowitz had not worn them before and, better still, it meant that no one with impetigo had worn them either. I thanked Stacie and even thought about hugging her (something people seemed to do a lot around here), but refrained when she reached around to scratch her rear.

I was ready for the trip.

to the tune of
"Tzena, Tzena, Tzena"

"Peanut butter, peanut butter,
Peanut butter, peanut butter
Peeee-nut butter, peanut butter

Peanut butter, peanut butter,
Peanut butter, peanut butter
Peeee-nut butter, peanut butter

Jelly! Jelly! Jelly, peanut butter
Peanut buuu-ter, peanut bu-u-u-ter
Jelly! Jelly! Jelly, peanut butter
Peanut buuu-ter, peanut bu-u-u-ter

Peach nectar, peach nectar, peanut butter
peanut butter
Peeee-nut butter, peanut butter
Peach nectar, peach nectar, peanut butter
peanut butter
Peeee-nut butter, peanut butter

Grapes! Grapes! Grapes, peanut butter
Peanut buuu-ter, peanut bu-u-u-ter
Grapes! Grapes! Grapes, peanut butter
Peanut buuu-ter, peanut bu-u-u-ter

Peanut butter, peanut butter,
Peanut butter, peanut butter
Peeee-nut butter, peanut butter

Peanut butter, peanut butter,
Peanut butter, peanut butter
Peeee-nut butter, SANDWICH DAY!"

8

WE WOULD BE RIDING TO MOUNT KATAHDIN IN THE GOOD TAN VAN. It was our one relatively safe and modern vehicle, purchased by Saul from a local mental hospital that went out of business and a point of contention between the girls' and boys' head counselors. Boys' Side already had the bigger waterfront, the less-buckled tennis courts, and the hotter bad food, so Jacques believed it was only right that they should also have the only decent transportation. And Wendy thought that that was just plain wrong. In the beginning of the summer, in an attempt to prove who needed it more, the two head counselors duked it out, each planning as many out-of-camp trips as possible necessitating the use of the van. For the boys, this meant canoeing through freshly sawn logs floating down the Kennebec River or trips to the newly modernized "air-cooled" bowling alley. For the girls it meant rides into Skowhegan where we could buy bandannas at Cut Price Clothing before heading into Woolworth's to fantasize about the percolators and place mats we'd purchase one day when we had our own kitchens.

The battle over the Good Tan Van grew so intense that Wendy and Jacques took to stealing it away from each other in the middle of the night. Ultimately, Jacques won the war simply because Wendy had no great desire to keep sending us out all the time. Her idea of a perfect day was one where everyone was together and busy. On the rare occasion when it was sunny, she would declare a Beach Day and we'd spend the whole morning and afternoon down at the lake. Jacques, on the other hand, liked Boys' Side best when it was empty and he could stay behind planning the next batch of activities, or whatever it was he and my counselor did in that back room.

Today, however, we'd be sharing the van as we set off to go climb a rock. The counselor on the trip was upstairs dining hall moaner Julie Printz, a dyed-in-the-wool Manhattanite whose closest experience to mountain climbing thus far was a class field trip to the Statue of Liberty in the early 1960s, when they still let you up into the crown. Used to taking taxis, she wasn't much of a driver either, and spent at least five minutes adjusting the seat and muttering things like, "What's this knob do?" before the rest of us boarded.

Kenny, the one experienced climber, rode shotgun, second in command. He took this trip and his position of authority very seriously, even more so than captaining the intercamp basketball team, and he'd brought along enough charts and maps to rival Magellan.

"So you're really into mountain climbing?" I asked, not really interested but hoping to make conversation.

"Yup, climbing's the best" was his reply, which of course would have to change if I had my way, married him in a few years, and we bought a house in the suburbs where I'd learn to play mah-jongg and make onion dip from a bag of Lipton soup mix.

The rest of us were seated in tighter quarters, squeezed together in the rear two rows of the van, crushed by all of the equipment. Our group included Mindy Plotke and a couple of boys from the now-burnt-down Wolverines' bunk. One of them, Keith Fernbach, lived in London, a wealthy kid whose parents thought it might be nice for him to get away from rainy London and spend eight weeks in sunny America. Oh well. Keith spent a lot of time complaining about the girl back home he'd recently broken up with, a "jolly hockey sticks what-ho" type. I had no idea if that was a good or bad type, I just liked listening to his accent. Marc Gross, from Rhode Island, was better known as "El Mosquito" because, well, he looked like one. The only boy I ever met who slept with his glasses on, Marc never had a nickname before he came to camp and was honored to go by the new moniker.

We'd driven about one hundred feet off the property when Julie realized she'd forgotten to get directions to the mountain, and Kenny's maps and charts were no good to us for another eighty-one miles. "Bloody hell!" Keith yelled out. Another thing that was great about having a Brit at camp was learning all of his swear words. Julie dropped us off at O'Boyle's while she went back for a map.

Everyone loved O'Boyle's. While most summer camps have a building designated as the Canteen, a place for socializing and buying snacks, Saul was too cheap to stock his own snack bar and staff it. Instead we shopped at the general store across the street, run by three family members whom we knew only as Ma, Pa, and Son O'Boyle. They dressed like we did, in overalls with bandannas, but they were serious. This little building was our oasis of candy and soda in Saul's desert of dreadful food. Rumor had it that the locals shopped here, too, which might explain who was buying the Schlitz beer and dented cans of pumpkin pie filling, but we rarely saw anyone from outside camp. In the summer it was like we owned the place and I couldn't fathom how the O'Boyles survived the winter without our patronage.

Mindy Plotke wondered about that, too.

"I'll bet they love us *and* they hate us," she stated.

"Why would they hate us?" I asked.

"Everyone hates it when the nouveau riche invade."

Mindy Plotke was not only pretty and petite, she was also really, really smart in a dark sort of way, the kind of person I thought my bunkmate Betty Gilbert could be friends with, if Betty ever looked up from her books while she was awake.

A few minutes and numerous junk food purchases later, Julie came back with a map—and Dana Bleckman. For the first time all summer, I wasn't pleased to see her.

"Changed my mind again," Dana announced as she held up her guitar. "You guys can squeeze me in, right?"

I wanted to say, "No, there's no room for you in the van and no room for you in Kenny's heart. Today it's all about me, me, me." But that would have made me look bad.

Dana tossed her gear on top of the rest of ours, squeezing into the back row. Kenny appeared more than a little annoyed, too, and I found that temporarily comforting.

Julie's lack of driving skills, coupled with our cramped circumstances, made the trip up the I-95 as uncomfortable as any ride in the Green Truck. In order to make it to the mountain and set up camp before nightfall, we didn't stop until we'd reached the town of Millinocket, home of the Great Northern Paper Company and the last vestige of civilization. The telephone and power lines ended here, so while refueling the van at Last Chance Gas, Julie decided to phone the camp and let them know we'd arrived safely. She placed a collect call, which the Main Office refused to accept.

As we headed down the Park Road, Katahdin came into view. Henry David Thoreau, whose masterpiece *Walden* would bore me to distraction in my sophomore-year English class at Brandeis University, wrote an essay on this mountain in which he described it as an example of "primeval, untamed and forever untamable nature." While everyone else in the van oohed and aahed, it was at this moment I knew it was not in my nature to enjoy nature. Forget Thoreau. As I looked up at this purple mountain's majesty, I recalled the legendary words of my great-grandmother Malka, as she wrapped her good candlesticks in an apron on the eve of her journey from Pinsk to Ellis Island: "Oy, such a schlep. Remind me why we're doing this again?"

Of course, one glance at Kenny and my heart flooded with the promise of the new world that lay ahead—if I could just survive the trip. The last six and a half miles of the van ride took us down a gravel road to Togue Pond Gate and the rangers' station. It was around four o'clock when we checked in and headed for the Roaring Brook campground.

"I think it's time for a nap," Dana announced and then yawned.

"How can you climb a mountain if you can't even ride in a car?" Kenny snapped. "Don't you think we should set up our tents and build a fire?"

"Well, okay, if I had any idea how to do that," she replied.

"I'm an Eagle Scout. I can do it," Kenny said.

"You're an Eagle Scout?" El Mosquito was surprised.

"Well, close," Kenny backpedaled. "Had a little run-in with the scoutmaster."

"How was that?" Keith laughed. "He ran into you smoking pot?"

Kenny reddened. "Wish my dad laughed that hard when he found out."

As it turned out, disqualified scout Kenny was the only one who knew how to do anything. I wanted to help, as an excuse to stay close by, but the best thing we could all do was keep out of the way. I joined the group over by the van where we broke open a bag of Chips Ahoy! cookies and watched the sun set over a mountain I prayed would disappear by morning.

"Girls, stop eating!" Kenny called over, once the fire was going. "I need you to come make dinner."

Now I'd always thought camping out meant cooking hot dogs and hamburgers, but the Kin-A-Hurra kitchen staff had supplied us with nothing but chicken parts and raw carrots, to be washed down with ten more industrial-size cans of peach nectar. I planned on filling my canteen from the lake.

Keith volunteered to cook, but right in the middle of the barbecue it started to rain. As each batch of poultry was freshly burnt, it was brought inside the girls' tent, which became our makeshift picnic ground. After we'd chowed down and strewn little wishbones all across our living space, it stopped raining and was time to go outside again, to build another fire and to do the thing I most couldn't do, sing.

Dana started us off with the requisite "Blowin' in the Wind." Taxed by the pressure of trying to look like I was singing when I was not, I decided to take a break after the first song.

"I need to go brush my teeth," I told Julie. "And maybe, if I have to," I gulped, "use the outhouse."

Julie the urbanite was as grossed out as I was. "They never show you that part on *Bonanza*," she complained. "They make it look like the Ponderosa was one big party."

Julie suggested I go with a buddy: "In case a moose or something attacked us."

"So if a moose attacks one of us, the other's supposed to save them?" I asked.

"Okay, never mind," said Julie. "Just go."

"I'll go with you," said Mindy Plotke. "In case a moose attacks you, I want to see that."

Now I am proud to say that I have never had a cavity, though it's not for lack of eating sugar. I simply brush my teeth. A lot. Though not as much as those people with the hand-washing issues. My buddy of the moment, Mindy Plotke, had that covered.

I spat out a mouhful of Colgate then swished a sip from my canteen.

"How can you drink that?" she asked me, then produced a bottle of clear liquid featuring a picture of a mountain peak.

"What's that?" I asked.

"Bottled water. I had my parents ship me a case."

"Bottled water? You paid for water?"

It was the dumbest thing I'd ever heard.

"It's so much purer," she explained as she unwrapped a cake of soap.

"Just seems a little weird."

"No, I'll tell you what's weird," Mindy Plotke said. "Those songs around the campfire. Don't you wonder why we always sing folk songs at camp?"

"Not really. We're at camp. This is what you sing."

"Yes, but why? Why these songs of longing and desperation? I smell fraud, don't you? I mean, aren't we essentially a bunch of rich, spoiled kids whose greatest worries in life are being picked last in gym class or wait-listed at Tufts?"

Mindy Plotke was the youngest captain in the history of her high school debate team and I was finding out why.

"American folk songs hearken back to the days of slavery," she went on, "but haven't we as Jews managed to avoid that since fleeing the pharaoh in favor of desk jobs? Where did we come off singing, 'All my trials, Lord, soon be over'? How do we identify with that?"

"Um. Uh . . ."

"Exactly," Mindy Plotke broke in, and then I think she had an epiphany or some other brain malfunction.

"Or wait a minute," she said. "On second thought, this *is* about the religion. At Jewish weddings, when the groom crushes a wine glass with his shoe, it's to commemorate the destruction of the Second Temple in Jerusalem because even in our greatest moments of joy, we must remember tragedy."

My mother told me the tragedy was breaking a perfectly good glass.

"Perhaps," she went on, "we sing folk songs at camp because even though things seem perfectly fine, as Jews, we're trained to anticipate disaster at any moment and then cling to some fleeting hope."

"And sing about it?" I asked. "I don't know . . ."

"But these songs aren't just for Jewish summer camps," she noted, "so maybe it's more of a widespread adolescent cry, a plea for a different kind of change, internal as opposed to external. With hormones raging out of control, coupled with an inability to understand what is happening to us, perhaps the only way to release the pent-up frustration and anxiety is by shaking our fists in the air and boldly screaming out, 'Yes! Someone's crying, Lord! Kum-Ba-Yah, dammit!'"

She was sure she was on to something.

"That must be it, right? Tell me I'm right. There is no other explanation."

I could think of one.

"Or maybe it's just because the words are easy to learn?"

Mindy Plotke was rendered speechless.

"You know my bunkmate Betty Gilbert?" I asked. "You two might be good as friends."

"That sleepwalking, book-reading freak?" Mindy P. exclaimed. "She hates camp. She doesn't get it."

"I just thought, y'know, you're both sort of afraid of germs and—"

I never got to finish. Mindy Plotke washed her hands of me and walked away.

Upon my return to the campfire, I found Dana leading the group in "You've Got a Friend." Standing apart from the others, listening and watching, I discovered I was pleased she'd brought along her guitar, regretting I'd been annoyed when she first showed up. I was out in the middle of nowhere with everything in my life in flux, but as one song segued into another, finally ending with "Goodnight Irene," all I could think was, *This is what camp is supposed to be like,* and I wanted the night to last forever.

It almost did last forever. I couldn't sleep. The ground was hard and uneven and no matter which way I turned it felt like rocks were growing under my sleeping bag. Around two a.m., I sat up straight when I heard the piercing cries of what sounded like victims in a bad Japanese monster movie. Had the prowlers followed us here?

"Relax, it's just loons," Dana said in the dark.

"Loons? You mean crazy people?"

"No. I mean loons."

Loons. Black-and-white-checked web-footed birds found in northern waters during the summer months. The wailing sounds were their method of communicating across long distances, much the way my mother would call to me when she was watching TV in the den and I was upstairs in my bedroom and she wanted a piece of rye bread from the kitchen.

By five a.m. I was growing restless. I pulled on the old pants I'd worn on the van ride and got up to take a walk. Just as I stepped outside, Julie woke up and screamed.

"Ahhhhh! Moose! It's a moose!"

Everyone else woke up and joined in the screaming.

"Moose! Moose!"

"Oh God! It's right outside the tent!"

"It's gonna kill us and eat us!"

I didn't see the moose but was terrified nonetheless. I dove back inside.

"Oh, it's just you," Julie said.

Everyone calmed down when they realized there was no moose, just me, standing outside in my brown painter's pants. I decided not to wear them again that summer.

The new day officially began at 5:30 a.m. with a breakfast of O'Boyle's leftovers. On a fresh sugar high, we packed up camp and set out. Kenny took on the task of hauling a bulky old canvas backpack containing assorted supplies. He looked uncomfortable and I was tempted to offer to share the load, but I didn't want to risk implying he was a weakling.

"Shouldn't someone help him?" I quietly asked Dana. "I mean, at least one of the other boys?"

"He loves this stuff," she assured me. "He thinks torture makes him look cool, like a junior Jim Norbert."

"You're so mean to him," I marveled.

"I almost didn't come on this trip because of him," Dana explained. "Like it's my fault I didn't want to be his girlfriend. Enough already. Get over it. Let him get some other girlfriend."

Yes, let him.

As Kenny struggled under the weight of his load, all I had to carry were my camera, flashlight, and canteen. There would be no stops along the way for refills, so the amount of water each of us had for the day was limited to roughly what your average Los Angeleno now consumes while crossing the parking lot from the Hummer to the Starbucks.

"So how do we do this, Julie? Where do we start?" Dana asked.

"Um, Kenny?" was her reply.

It was obvious who would be in charge here.

"As long as we stick to the most popular route, Chimney Pond Trail, nothing will go wrong," Kenny assured us. Flashlights on, we trudged through the dark over loose, craggy rock and gravel for two hours.

"This isn't so bad," I said to Dana. "I'll bet we're almost there."

"Congratulations," Kenny announced when we reached Chimney Pond, "we are now officially at the beginning of the hike."

It was pointless to complain. Julie had that covered.

"The beginning? So why didn't we drive here?"

"Because there's no roads," Kenny told her. "And the whole point is to hike. Remember? That's why we're here."

Once we'd passed through a quarter mile of scrub, we emerged to find the view had changed. The sun was now shining brightly on Mount Katahdin, though we could not yet see the peak. What we saw was a steep wall of boulders. The next phase of the trip, Cathedral Trail, was the most direct route to the top that didn't involve crampons and ropes and scaling the face of the mountain. During the drive, Kenny had read through a booklet about Katahdin and now pulled it from his back pocket, happily providing us with information.

"A sudden and unexpected slide in 1967 wiped out a significant portion of this trail."

"How do we know there won't be another slide today?" Julie asked.

"Pardon, but for a group leader, you're not very reassuring," Keith remarked.

Kenny skimmed ahead. "Says here Cathedral Trail got its name from the vertical slabs of rock that jut out. Supposed to remind hikers of cathedral spires."

"Oh, please," whined Julie, "the vertical slabs of rock that jut out remind me that we'll be spending the next few hours climbing over vertical slabs of rock that jut out."

Despite my borrowed dungaree-induced restricted knee movement, I'd easily been able to keep up so far. As Kenny reached over his head and found a place to grab on to the first boulder, I brushed past the boys from the Wolverines and made myself second in line. I was about to tap Kenny on the shoulder, check in, say hi, and offer some words of encouragement, hoping in turn he'd notice my facility for mountain climbing and ask me to be his date for the Banquet Social at the end of the summer. Instead, he lost his footing and rebalanced himself by pushing his left boot against my head.

Kenny looked back. "Oh, it's you," he said, then squinted in the sun. "Why do you look different?"

Ah, good, he'd noticed. I was afraid I hadn't taken extreme enough measures when I'd opted not to address the lack of knockers problem. I was still a double-A, a size sometimes referred to as a "training bra," as if I somehow needed more practice before signing up for the official Boob Olympics. I'd heard that a couple of Stay-Free Maxi Pads wedged into your bra could do the trick, but even with their handy dandy self-adhesive strip, I couldn't imagine how they'd remain in place during a daylong hike or that they'd feel particularly comfortable.

The truth was, I liked my small chest. I was an athlete and it seemed so convenient. Wouldn't double-Ds get in the way if I was up at bat in a crucial late inning, trying to pull the ball to right? I'd always thought these were the two best parts of my body, if I really had to think about them. Along with my ears. I had pretty good ears, if anyone was looking, which they weren't because I didn't wear earrings because my mother considered piercing cannibalistic and I probably would have been losing them all the time anyway and then my parents would yell at me, so really, why bother in the first place? But I thought my ears were pretty good nonetheless. Nice and petite. All I ever really wanted was for the rest of my body to have been built to match.

I tried to be subtle as I declared to Kenny, "I'm outdoorsy."

"No, that's not it," he said. "Oh, it's because I'm standing above you. You don't look so tall."

I should have stuffed my bra.

Rather than dwell on how far away and unachievable my ultimate goal remained, I focused on climbing each individual stone, one at a time, the way baseball managers tell their players to go for singles and not home runs. And although I was a part of a group, within a short time I envisioned myself alone, falling into a trance-like state, pulling myself up rock after rock. It went on like this until the climb began to feel effortless, as if I could go on this way indefinitely. And then, about forty-five minutes later, the spell was broken when half a dozen nuns in full habits and Converse sneakers pushed past us, mumbling something about how slowly we were moving. Shortly after that we reached flat ground.

"Are we there yet?" Mindy Plotke asked, running out of breath.

"Yes," Kenny replied, "we've reached the top of the Lower Cathedral."

"Lower? You mean there are *two*?" El Mosquito asked in shock.

"No," said Kenny. "Three. Lower, Middle, and Upper Cathedral."

There are times in your life when you just don't want to accept what you know is true, like the Beatles breaking up or your first cell phone bill.

"And then?" Julie asked hopefully.

"And then we begin our ascent to the top."

This was one of those times.

"Am I the only one who wants to be here?" Kenny asked.

No one answered.

"Okay, I know you said there's no place to refill our canteens," Dana noted, "but do you think we might pass a soda machine?"

We were well above the tree line and could feel the air getting thinner. As we advanced, Mindy Plotke fell farther and farther behind. Kenny suggested she climb up front with him so he could keep an eye on her, and I spent the next three hours and two cathedrals reaching the tops of boulders only to catch a glimpse of Miss Plotke's tiny butt. This meant Keith Fernbach, behind me, was spending the day watching my larger derriere breaking in Stacie's Levi's and I was thankful she'd let me ink out the waist size on the back tag.

"All we have to do now," Kenny told us at the top of the trail, "is take the cathedral cutoff, cross the boulder field to Saddle Trail, and then go up to the top."

"And then get back down," Julie groaned.

By early afternoon we saw it—Baxter Peak. The highest point in Maine was just a quarter mile away. But like Dorothy and friends, who could see the Emerald City yet struggled across the poppy field, the last part of our journey was the toughest. There were no more boulders to wrestle, just tiny shards of rock to cross that made your ankles twist and turn and feel like they were breaking with each step. Everyone but Kenny slipped and tripped on the loose rocks, whining all the way that we'd never get there. Then inspiration came. I'd like to say it was in the form of the six nuns on their way back down who shouted, "You can do it, kids," but it was really the group that came down after them. A bunch of eight-year-olds in open-toed sandals were pointing and snickering in a foreign language. Though it was not English, the translation was obvious: "wimps." When we reached the top, Kenny called out "Lunch!" and dumped out the backpack. It was full of peanut butter and jelly sandwiches, the ones we'd refused on yesterday's van ride. This time, we ate them.

I was the only one in the group who felt compelled to climb the thirteen-foot rock pile.

"Doesn't anybody else want to say they did it?" I asked.

"Bloody hell, we just climbed a whole mountain," sighed Keith. "Isn't that enough?"

"Want me to take a picture?" Dana offered.

The view from the top of Maine should have been astounding, but when I looked out I couldn't see a thing. A cloud had blown over the peak. Kenny hadn't read us the part of the booklet detailing the mountain's sudden climate changes, its hazardous conditions, and the number of people who'd met their deaths on Baxter Peak. At someone's suggestion, we stood still until it passed, giggling in the dense, wet fog. Julie, who couldn't see her hand in front of her face, became giddy and broke into a chorus of "I Can See Clearly Now." The cloud passed after a few minutes and more pictures were taken.

"Maybe you should take a rock from the pile as a souvenir," Dana called out as I climbed down.

This seemed like a good idea. Maybe I'd take two, one for me and one for Hallie. Flat ones for our noses.

"What're you telling her?" Kenny asked in horror. "You can't take them. This is a national park. You can't take anything."

"Oh, I didn't . . ." I stammered.

"That pile's been there since, like, 1900. If everybody who climbed up here took one, it wouldn't be here anymore," Kenny scolded. "I swear, you girls'll ruin this mountain for everyone."

"I'm sorry," I said. "I didn't know."

Kenny saw me toss the rocks back, gave a satisfied look, and said, "That's better," which I interpreted as forgiveness because I needed to believe he'd forgiven me. What he didn't see was that as soon as he turned away, Dana made a face at him, retrieved two rocks, and tucked them into my canteen pouch. I let them stay there.

Had I paid any attention thus far this summer to my fellow campers' tales of Katahdin, I would have known that, after reaching Baxter Peak, you don't just turn around and go back down. Instead, we would now follow the trail connecting Baxter Peak with Pamola Peak, which required crossing the notorious mile-and-a-half Knife Edge trail.

"This part's a little treacherous," Kenny warned us.

I didn't see what the big deal was. Yes, if you fell off it was a steep drop of a few thousand feet, but it didn't seem like a problem since the path was easily thirty feet wide—until you reached the part where it was just three feet across and the footing only half of that. Everyone stopped and looked down.

"Isn't this the cliff Wile E. Coyote keeps falling off of in the *Road Runner* cartoons?" I asked.

Julie Printz, long since retired as our leader, screamed.

"What?" I said. "It's just a cartoon. He doesn't die."

This was when we found out why Julie had enjoyed the cloud cover on Baxter Peak. With the exception of the escalators at Bloomingdale's, she was terrified of heights.

"I thought this trip would help me get over it," she whimpered, frozen in her tracks. "You know, what doesn't kill you, makes you stronger?"

"And how are you feeling now?" El Mosquito asked.

"Not stronger," was her quiet reply.

"Oh, come on, it's no big deal. It's not like there's bees," Dana said and skipped across.

Keith Fernbach was next to traverse the narrow section, screaming his signature catchphrase. As the rest of us followed, we each momentarily became British, yelling out, "Bloody hell!" until we'd crossed to where the trail widened out again. All of us, that is, except Julie, who was now down on her hands and knees.

"What if I crawl across?" she asked, hyperventilating.

Kenny held his hands out in front of him, making a quick measurement of Julie's body width.

"Wouldn't try it," he said. "Right over the side if the wind blows."

"You're not helping," Dana snapped.

Julie was sobbing now, but I was pleased. Pleased that Dana and Kenny were not getting along.

"Isn't she, like, the counselor?" El Mosquito asked.

"Okay, that's it," Kenny announced. "We've gotta go back."

"No! No!" Julie called out. "If I don't get over it now, I'll be afraid my whole life! I have to do this!"

"I can do this, I can do this," became her new mantra. She was the new Little Engine That Could. Only she couldn't, and what should have been a five-hour hike down the mountain began to feel as miscalculated as Gilligan's three-hour tour. Other groups of hikers excused themselves and walked around Julie.

"I know I can do this," Julie told herself aloud.

"Yeah, okay, but when?" was Kenny's impatient response.

It looked as though things might get ugly until Dana came up with the musical answer: "She'll be comin' round the mountain when she comes," she sang and was immediately joined by everyone else, except for me.

We probably should have been coming up with words of encouragement for Julie, but it was more fun to come up with songs that contained the word "mountain" and the group segued into "The Bear Went Over the Mountain" followed by "Rocky Mountain High."

"What are you doing?" Kenny screamed.

"Can't help it, pal," Dana shouted back. "The hills are alive."

Dana spun around in circles, giddy, reprising Borscha
Belyavsky's Russian-accented version of "Climb Ev'ry Mountain"
as Kenny stalked off some twenty feet, turned his back to us, and
sat down on a rock.

This left me in a hard place. I could go to him or I could stay
with the group—and sing. With the altitude as an excuse for my
limited vocal range, I dug deep down and helped belt out "The Big
Rock Candy Mountain," "On Top of Spaghetti" (which, we found
out too late, does not contain the word "mountain"), and finally
the Kin-A-Hurra attempt at a soulful version of "Ain't No Mountain High Enough."

Julie, calling out to us, still hadn't moved, but the rest of us
were rocking. As we faux–Motown danced along the ridge, the sun
went down on our second day at Katahdin. All of the other hikers
were long gone by now.

Julie grew calmer in the dark. As it turned out, since she could
no longer see the drop, her fear of heights receded. "If we'd known,"
I said, "we could've blindfolded her hours ago and been done by
now."

When she finally walked across the Knife Edge and rejoined
the rest of the group, we applauded her performance, hugged, and
broke into "Taps."

"Day is done

Gone the sun."

Kenny shined his flashlight our way. "Might want to save it,"
he barked. "Be a good idea to get down before the temperature
drops below freezing."

We soon learned that, aside from the freezing temperatures, a
good reason not to climb at night is that you can't see the markers
on the trail. Even with all of our flashlights on, there was a chance
we might end up stranded or worse. We chose "worse."

"I think I'm slipping . . ."

"What? Mindy, you say something?" El Mosquito asked.

"I said I think I'm—"

And that was the last we heard from Mindy Plotke.

I'm pretty sure we were off the beaten path when she slid on loose gravel, knocked over El Mosquito, and then tumbled some thirty feet, fracturing her ankle and bumping her head on a rock before disappearing into the brush.

Kenny was an Eagle Scout, sort of, and I was certain he'd know what to do. He grabbed me by the shoulders and pulled me close. It seemed like an odd time for a first kiss. "What do we do? What do we do? What do we do?" he yelled frantically.

Julie grabbed Kenny, pulled the first-aid kit from his backpack, and then went looking for our missing camper. I peered down the trail, not knowing what I was looking for, but found it anyway. We were a mere hundred yards from the rangers' station and one of the rangers was running uphill toward us. Seems we'd been reported missing hours earlier. Ranger Bob radioed for an ambulance and Mindy P., who'd landed nearby, came to shortly after the paramedics arrived.

"Well," said Dana as the flashing lights and siren signaled the debate team captain's departure, "this was memorable. I can see why everyone makes a point of signing up for this swell trip."

Most of the other campers fell asleep as soon as we hit the road and the trip back to camp was fairly quiet. It was dark in the van and somewhere around the town of Hinckley, I thought about slipping out of Stacie's stiff pants, only to realize that they were now fully broken in. Soft and comfortable, the best pants I'd ever worn, and tomorrow I would have to give them back.

"Mindy," someone whispered in my direction.

It was Kenny, scrambling over a sleeping camper to sit by my side.

"You know, you did pretty good up there."

"I did? You think?"

"You're a good climber. And you stayed really calm. You know, at the end there."

"Yeah, well, and you . . ." I stopped myself.

Kenny looked sheepish. "Guess the pressure of the responsibility got to me a little."

Kenny Uber was confiding in me, admitting he wasn't perfect. This could be progress. This could be promising.

I had to ask. "You still mad Dana came along? You still like her?"

"That witch with a B? No way. You wish Philip had come?"

"Philip?"

"He's your boyfriend, isn't he?"

"For like a day. It's nothing. It doesn't count," I told him, then worried that maybe I should have stuck with the hard-to-get routine.

"So can you believe Jim called this 'a fine little hike'?" Kenny laughed. "I'll have to have a talk with him."

"Yeah."

"Hey, could you do me a favor?" Kenny asked.

"Okay."

"About what happened back there? You don't have to tell anyone. I'm sure Dana will, but you could deny it."

Of course I would, because he still had his pride and I still had my hopes up. I was head over heels, though not literally like Mindy Plotke, and Kenny was starting to see me as a friend. Climbing the mountain had not been a waste of time, for in the process I had jumped a small hurdle.

Oh, and I got to sing.

to the tune of "Oom-pah-pah"
from the musical Oliver!

"<GASP> <COUGH COUGH>
<GASP> <COUGH COUGH>
That's how it goes,
When you hear the Green Truck
Go down the road
Carbon monoxide goes right up your nose
When you hear <GASP> <COUGH COUGH>"

9

A FEW DAYS AFTER THE RETURN FROM KATAHDIN, SAUL RATTNER showed up for breakfast on Girls' Side. Standing in the middle of the dining room, puffing on his pipe, Saul slowly waved his right hand in a downward motion to shush us. Betty Gilbert helped him out.

"Shut up! Saul wants to talk."

"Thank you, sweetie," he smiled at her. Saul had a habit of calling all the campers "Honey" or "Sweetie," which I suspected was less a term of endearment than an excuse not to learn anybody's name.

"I have a wonderful announcement to make," our camp director told us. "The prowlers have been captured and sent to jail."

I think he was expecting joy and jubilation, but for the most part no one seemed to care. The acts of prowling had become something of a letdown, as the intruders shied away from throwing rocks and shouting into bunk windows, settling instead for late night swims and occasionally stealing a towel off the clothesline. The prowlers had no real impact on us anymore. They were just another part of camp, one we rarely saw. Kind of like Saul.

For me, the bigger news was that there were no little boxes of Kellogg's Sugar Frosted Flakes on the table this morning. In their place were simpler, old-fashioned-looking packages, some wheat flake cereal called Pep.

"Vhat happened to our cereal?" Borscha called out. She had adapted well to American junk food.

"Glad you asked," said Saul. "Has anyone here been following the national news?"

The only news we'd been following was who got a package in the mail, who got a hickey, and who had the scabbiest mosquito bites. Nothing fit to print.

"There was an article," Saul continued, "stating that sugary breakfast cereals are not very healthy. So we're not going to have them anymore."

No more sugarcoated cereal? I nearly lost my will to live but then I remembered about Kenny.

"We're going to try something new," he explained.

"This is new?" Dana questioned. "It looks antique."

"Autumn Evening," I said, nudging her, "do you remember eating this cereal in a past life?"

"Yes, in the eighteen hundreds, when I was shipwrecked in the Caribbean and it was all we had aboard," she answered. "Arghh, matey, shiver ye Pep."

"Really?"

"No. Why are you asking?"

I was asking because it clicked in my head why this unfamiliar cereal looked so familiar. I'd seen a carton of Pep in the closet under the stairs over on Boys' Side. Was Saul serving us breakfast cereal from the 1940s?

"They're just like Wheaties," Saul explained as he released a plume of smoke. "Very good for you."

While I debated revealing to my bunkmates that this cold cereal might predate the Cold War, Saul informed us of current world events. He had a habit of making everything he said sound like a sermon, which meant most of us stopped paying attention around the third or fourth sentence.

During a particularly lengthy diatribe on the high price of eggs, the pay phone at the front of the dining room rang. It was Mindy Plotke calling from her bedroom in Florida with an update on her broken ankle and the gash in her head that had required fifteen stitches. "It's so agonizingly boring!" was what she had to say, and the information was relayed to the rest of us. "I've been lying in bed for three days, staring out the window and watching the heat rise on the driveway."

Mindy Plotke came from substantial wealth. Her parents had picked her up from the hospital in Millinocket and flown her home in a private jet, back to their house in the hideous southern summer heat. I thought the wealth and jet parts were pretty cool, but her current situation was as anticlimactic as the prowlers' capture. "I can't tolerate it anymore," she went on. "And my parents say I'm driving them berserk, so I'm coming back."

Rather than refund Mr. and Mrs. Plotke's money, Saul assured them that the camp nurse could take care of their daughter in the well-equipped girls' infirmary. Her parents had never seen the camp, so they acquiesced to Mindy P.'s wishes. With a cast on her leg, stitches in her head, and instructions that neither could get wet, Mindy Plotke returned via commercial jet. Junior counselor Connie Pechman picked her up at Bangor International Airport in Connie's yellow 1968 VW Beetle. Connie had spent a good deal of the summer extremely itchy because she was allergic to the seaweed in the lake. To combat a full body rash, she was given a prescription for a medication that made her extremely groggy. To counteract the grogginess, she was given a prescription for speed, which made her extremely popular with the rest of the staff.

Security was somewhat lax at the Bangor hangar and no one noticed that after loading her convalescent charge into the VW Connie hoisted the wheelchair—with its big Delta Airlines logo on the side—onto the roof of the Bug, strapped it down, and drove off. The plan was to wheel Mindy Plotke around camp for the rest of the summer, but the dirt roads were rocky and bumpy when it wasn't raining and pure mud when it was, so mostly people just carried her around. I hated how the boys fought over who'd get to give her a piggyback ride, noting that she "barely weighed a pound," but on the plus side this freed up the wheelchair for other purposes.

Camp was not at full capacity and Bunk Six was empty. It was used as storage for trunks, many of which were filled with campers' and counselors' stashes of junk food from O'Boyle's and care packages from generous parents. My trunk contained stationery with envelopes preaddressed to relatives and a sewing kit, in case my name tags came loose. Mindy Plotke's bunkmates arranged the trunks into a maze and created a game called Obstacle Course. A camper, blindfolded with a bandanna, would sit in the chair and be pushed at high speeds through the labyrinth. It was a stupid game that was especially popular when the boys came over to visit because it somehow led to people having to touch each other.

For true daredevils, there was Roller Coaster. Norit Ben-Sorek, a camper from Jerusalem and a future sergeant in the Israeli Defense Force, dreamed up this one. The wheelchair was brought to the top of the rocky road leading to the Havens where a brave camper would take the seat.

"I will count to three," Norit explained, "and then I will let go."

"I'll do it," Autumn Evening volunteered and sat down. "Count away!"

"*Echad, shtayim, shalosh!*" Norit counted off in Hebrew, then she pushed with her foot, sending Autumn Evening crashing out of control, down the dirt road and into the sticker bushes.

"That was incredible! I have to do that again," my bunkmate announced, climbing out of the brush and back up the hill.

I didn't particularly enjoy Roller Coaster, but I didn't want anyone to know I was afraid so I did it three times.

Mindy Plotke got special treatment on the day we went to Rummel's in Waterville. Home of a miniature golf course and the Icky Orgy, a concoction you created at the make-your-own-sundae bar, an evening at Rummel's was a much-anticipated annual event. Three bunks' worth of male and female campers and counselors—about fifty of us in all—crowded into the back of the Green Truck. Mindy Plotke, unable to climb up, got to ride in the cab with barely-English-speaking counselor Lars Snorth. Lars, who wore glasses comprised of one thick lens and one blacked-out lens, loved to drive Saul's vehicles as a means of proving it didn't matter that he was born missing his left eye and had only limited vision in the right. He especially enjoyed the challenge of changing lanes with the truck.

"Ugh, golf," Dana whined. "More exercise. Wasn't Katahdin enough? Will it never end?" Uninterested in the planned festivities, songstress Dana had brought along her guitar, planning to serenade us through the nine holes of fake golf. It didn't take much to convince her to also play on the way there. As passing motorists stared at our cargo of campers, we mooed along to "Take Me Home, Country Roads."

Every year, right around Rummel's time, someone would come up with the ingenious notion of covering the floor of the truck with some of the old cotton-covered blue-and-white-ticking mattresses.

"Again? Who put the mattresses in?" Maddy wanted to know.

"The boys did it. Why? It's not a good idea?" Hallie asked. "Won't it make the ride softer?"

"Softer—and wetter."

Because every year the rain would blow in through the slatted sides of the truck, soaking them. So tonight, this country road took us to Rummel's on soggy mattresses and we arrived with wet backsides, but not even that could dampen my spirits when I was in the vicinity of hot fudge sauce.

After polishing off my Icky Orgy, with just enough restraint to keep from licking the bowl in front of people, I should have felt sick. Instead, I felt ready for golf. As Philip's perceived girlfriend, I couldn't avoid partnering with him, but there was also nothing stopping me from inviting Autumn Evening and Kenny to join us.

"I'm really good at miniature golf," Philip informed me.

"That's too bad," I said. "I stink."

Even so, Autumn Evening, Philip, Kenny, and I seemed like the ideal foursome. Autumn Evening wasn't interested in Kenny, I wasn't interested in Philip, and Dana wasn't interested in participating. She sat on the sidelines next to Mindy Plotke, who was having her cast signed, and performed the entire Carole King album *Tapestry*, except for "Smackwater Jack," which nobody really likes.

By the fourth hole Kenny was two under par. "This is how a man plays," he gloated. I knew this was a shot at Philip who had not yet had his bar mitzvah and was still, technically, a boy.

Autumn Evening and I fell further and further behind and drifted into a conversation about how they made those mini golf mini pencils.

"Do you think they start out regular size then break them in two and sharpen both?" she asked. "Or do they just start out smaller?"

"These are just like the pencils at my house," I told her. "Except ours start out bigger and with erasers, until my brother Mark bites them off."

"Your brother eats pencil erasers?"

"All of them. It's so frustrating. It's like you can never make a mistake in our house."

The competition intensified between Philip and Kenny and they were tied going into the final hole.

"It all comes down to this last shot," Philip whispered, like a TV golf announcer. "Ladies and gentlemen, if either player can putt into the hippo's mouth, he will secure his place in history."

"Shut up, I'm trying to concentrate," Kenny snapped.

But Kenny and Philip both missed.

Autumn Evening skipped the hole. "I played so much golf in my last life," she said. "Who needs this?"

I went with my usual strategy: I closed my eyes and smacked the ball. Somehow, it went in.

"Lucky shot," Kenny snorted.

"You just won a free game," Philip informed me, and for the first time I think I heard slight irritation in his voice.

Thankfully, there was no time to play another round. We turned in our equipment and headed back to the Green Truck just as a strong wind was picking up.

"I don't feel good," one camper moaned five minutes after we hit the road.

"Maybe you had too much ice cream," a counselor suggested.

It was not the dessert in his belly that was doing the damage. It was the wind outside the truck that posed the problem. Per its design, the truck gave out massive amounts of carbon monoxide, which ordinarily blew out the tailpipe and affected only the unfortunate souls riding behind us. Tonight, however, the wind was blowing in the same direction we were traveling, whipping the noxious fumes back into the truck and into our lungs. It didn't take long for many other campers to grow nauseous. A couple even passed out.

Mindy Plotke, resting her cast on the cab dashboard, noticed we'd stopped singing "Great Big Globs of Greasy Grimy Gopher Guts" and peeked around into the back. Seeing something was horribly wrong, she grabbed Lars's arm, causing the truck to swerve. He regained control and pulled over.

By this time, Kenny was among the unconscious. *It's like a dream come true*, I thought to myself. If I gave him mouth-to-mouth resuscitation, I could bring him back to life. Except that I didn't know mouth-to-mouth. *But even if I screw up and he dies, he'll still be the first boy I ever kissed.* I began crawling over toward Kenny until Autumn Evening foiled my plan, getting to him first.

My bunkmate had told us weeks ago that she wasn't looking for a boyfriend this summer, but she had been spending a lot of time with Kenny ever since the play. I assumed they were just friends, that she was probably consoling him on losing Dana to Aaron. And she was doing mouth-to-mouth because she learned it in Junior Lifesaving. Advanced Beginners like myself never got to that.

The easiest thing would have been to find a pay phone, call the camp office, and have them send some other vehicles and maybe a nurse. But there were no pay phones around and the high winds had already knocked out the lines anyway.

Watching Autumn Evening attempt to breathe life back into Kenny gave my faux beau an idea and the once robust Philip suddenly passed out by my side. "Cut it out," I said. "I know you're faking." But if he wasn't, I was still the closest person to him who wasn't unconscious. I had to give him mouth-to-mouth even though I didn't know what I was doing. And if I couldn't do it right, I was still obligated to make it look like I cared.

I leaned in close to put my lips on his, worried that if I did manage to save him there was still the risk our braces might lock in some weird Chang and Eng Siamese dental horror show.

"A-choo!" The perfectly healthy Philip accidentally sneezed in my face. It was the most disgusting thing that had ever happened to me, but the timing couldn't have been better.

"Sorry," he whispered, truly remorseful as I wiped my face on my sleeve.

"It's okay," I replied, totally meaning it.

Lars swung open the back gates. "Everybody out!" he screamed into the wind.

Those who were able climbed out while the rest were assisted and we huddled by the side of the road, too cold to sing, and waited for someone to come up with a plan. No one did, but half an hour later everyone was able to breathe and the truck was poison-free.

This became the way to get home. Lars drove the truck as fast and as far as he could, fifteen minutes at a stretch, and then he'd pull over again. Bingeing and purging on carbon monoxide, the half hour trip back to camp took four hours and twenty minutes. It was the second-worst road trip I'd been on so far this year.

Six months earlier, in January of 1974, my father had a convention to attend in Orlando, Florida, and decided to bring the whole family along, turning it into a trip to Disney World. It was hard to believe this was really happening. We even got to miss school. My parents had been to Disneyland in 1967, when my father attended a convention in Los Angeles, but while they rode the Matterhorn and the Teacups, Mark, Jay, and I (David wasn't born yet) stayed in New Jersey with our grandmother. As a souvenir, my mother brought me back a colorful map of the park, which I took to school for Show and Tell, regaling my classmates with stories of what a wonderful time my parents had had without me.

No matter that January 1974 was the height of the Arab oil embargo. We loaded up the Custom Cruiser with suitcases and barf bags and drove from the Garden State to the Sunshine State. Heading south on I-95, you can't miss the miles and miles of signs for Mexican-themed South of the Border, an attraction in Dillon, South Carolina, open twenty-four hours a day, every day of the year. I knew of South of the Border from our neighbors, the Zemels, who had bumper stickers on their Buick Electra advertising the restaurants, attractions, stores, and campgrounds of the utopia that is South of the Border. They stopped there every year and stayed overnight in the three-hundred-room motel. Taking a cue from old-time Burma-Shave signs, the one hundred and twenty clever billboard ads ("You're always a wiener at Pedro's!" "Yule love us — even at Chanukkah!") began cropping up a hundred miles north, building anticipation and nearly brainwashing motorists into forgetting that South of the Border was not the final destination. My parents, however, were not fooled.

"We're not stopping?" I asked in dismay.

"There's nothing there," my mother said. "It's not for us."

"Not for us?"

I knew the food wouldn't be kosher but the whole place? As Jay turned his usual shade of green and puked, we passed a sign that read, "Keep yelling, kids! They'll stop!" But we kept on driving, south of South of the Border.

Surely we were the only family in America that didn't venture in, opting instead to arrive in Orlando on a Sunday afternoon, sweaty, cramped, exhausted, and with an empty gas tank. No open gas stations were to be found so my mother screamed at my father like this was his fault. Disney World was fun, but we knew that the ride back home would not be. In the end it was the car trip and not the Country Bear Jamboree that stuck out in my memory of our trip to the Happiest Place on Earth.

Lars drove the Green Truck directly to Saul's house, but only the sickest campers were to be dropped off and sent inside. Thanks to a deviated septum, my unique breathing pattern had left me unaffected by the carbon monoxide. Still, I was determined to tour the perfect little cabin on the edge of the lake. I coughed a few times and was allowed in. It was like walking into a woodsy wonderland catalog showroom. Saul had built himself a cocoon of comfort nestled amid the dreck he had provided the rest of us. I found myself both admiring and resenting him by the time I headed back out the front door a few minutes later, claiming a speedy recovery.

Kenny was among those dropped off to stay, to be checked out by the camp doctor, a podiatrist by trade. Outside, Philip was still ducking me as the boys were broken up into smaller groups and taken in several Good Tan Vanloads to nearby Boys' Side. The girls were crammed into the Valiant and the Food and Garbage Truck for the longer ride back to our side of the lake. I rode next to Autumn Evening.

Smushed close against her, I leaned in and asked, "What was it like giving Kenny mouth-to-mouth? Was it gross?"

"No," she assured me. "It wasn't so bad. We've been making out for the last two weeks."

Shaken, I asked, "What happened to not having a boyfriend this summer?"

"Oh, we're not going out," Autumn Evening explained. "It's just that there's nobody good available, so we're using each other to stay in practice. He's a pretty good kisser. I'll bet he was really sexy in a former life."

Back on Girls' Side, my bunkmates were too excited about the adventure to go to sleep, so they stayed up talking and playing music all night. I, however, crawled into bed under my mother's old green army blankets. Suddenly, I wasn't feeling so well.

"Hello Muddah, Hello Faddah . . ."

1 0

AN EIGHT-WEEK SUMMER CAMP IS LIKE A TANK OF GAS. IN THE beginning, you feel like it will last forever and then, as if without warning, it's halfway gone and you find yourself worrying that it'll run out on you before you've reached your destination.

The halfway markers were all in place: my counselor had lost three flashlights and four rain ponchos, the Arts & Crafts shack was out of beads, and everyone was talking about some big canoe trip coming up. Jim Norbert, who would be leading the adventure, came over to Girls' Side and presented his Vacationland vacation slides in the dining room.

My own family's vacations were not well documented. The Polaroid camera was big and bulky and all the fresh photos had to be laid out on a table and coated with this Chapstick-looking stuff so they wouldn't curl up. It was easier to take along the Bell & Howell 8mm motion picture camera and, when we got back home, mail away the film to be developed. Weeks later, when the plastic reel in the yellow box came back, my parents would set up the movie screen and projector in the den. My brothers and I would take our seats on the green vinyl couch while my father ran the projector and my mother sat behind it, catching the film in her hands because the take-up reel didn't work. The show was always the same—a grave disappointment.

The camera operated via a key-wind device on the side, like a music box or a 1910 jalopy, and my father, the family's official cameraman, never quite got the hang of it, having no idea when it was actually running. A high percentage of the film my father thought he shot turned out blank, while our most successful home movies were taken with the camera unmanned, left resting on a car seat and aimed at the dashboard or lying on the front hall steps, filming the closed front door. And on the occasions when there was an image my father had intended to record, it was usually my brothers and me standing around bored at yet another Colonial restoration.

"This he-yah is Dead Rivah," Jim Norbert announced as he clicked on the next slide. Jim, standing paddle in hand at the stern, looked like a yokel George Washington leading his troops across the Delaware. Only these troops were heading straight into the rapids, and the girls around me were lapping it up. The next few slides showed more whitewater rapids and one group of wet boys and girls who'd fallen out of their vessel going over a steep drop. The campers in the slide were laughing, and so were the campers around me. "He-yah's Moose Riv-ah, he-yah's the Penobscot," Jim continued, clicking through tens of similar scenes.

The slides of the Allagash River, site of the upcoming trip, drew the loudest cheers. For the past two weeks, every morning at five, several junior counselor girls had been running down to the lake, rain or shine (mostly rain), to practice their strokes. Around six a.m., they'd head back up to their bunks, chanting, as if possessed, "Allagash! Allagash!" And I thought I was nuts getting up early just to jog to Boys' Side with my counselor.

"What's so great about the Allagash?" I asked Maddy the morning after the slide show between gasps for air.

After four weeks of jogging, Maddy was firm and toned. I was still new at this and still a chocoholic, undoing all my early morning hard work by midafternoon.

"It's amazing," she told me. "You go through some of the roughest waters in Maine."

"You mean on purpose?"

"Yes, of course," she said. "It's magnificent. You start at Lake Telos, which is northwest of Katahdin, and you hook up with the Allagash, which eventually joins up with the St. John before it goes out to sea."

"The sea? What sea?"

"What do you mean 'what sea'? The sea."

"Like in that song?"

"What song? The sea that goes to the ocean. What's the difference?"

"Just asking."

"Anyway," Maddy continued, "it takes about ten days."

Ten days with ten campers led by Jim, camping, cooking, canoeing, and (according to rumors Maddy refused to confirm for me) sometimes losing their virginity to each other while Jim looked the other way. Because the entire route went through remote country, it was necessary to purchase all the supplies in advance and carry them in the canoes. If the sleeping bags or food or matches to build campfires got wet, you were up a well-known creek whether you had your paddle or not. This was the trip everyone dreamed of going on. Canoes. Jim Norbert. Peril.

"And that's—fun?" I asked.

"Yes, well, no. Well . . . if you like that sort of thing."

Maddy slowed down the pace and tried to explain.

"Think of it like this: it's the culmination of your years at camp. Most campers don't come back as counselors, like me. The Allagash is it. It's your graduation or your bar mitzvah of camp, one last shot at real physical exertion before law school or med school or some boring desk job. Get it?"

No, I didn't. "How much does this desk job pay?" I asked. "Do you have to type?"

"And," she added, "you get to have the paddle forever."

This part I understood. Before setting out, each participant got his or her own custom-made Old Town brand canoe paddle, which everyone on the trip autographed at the end with a permanent marker. I loved souvenirs and this was the ultimate. Had I known about the paddle, I might have considered brushing up on my strokes and trying out, only to have had my parents rummage around in the Horowitzes' garage and come up with some splintery old board for me to use instead.

By the time we arrived at Boys' Side, the sun was blazing overhead, the clearest day we'd seen all summer. I took a seat on the front steps of the office while Jacques and Maddy did whatever they did inside. Only five minutes had passed when a very cool-looking man and woman walked up. They didn't exactly look like adults—at least not the kind I knew in New Jersey—but they were way too ancient to be counselors. Maybe forty. Both of them wore flowing, gauzy clothes and granny glasses, like they'd walked off the cover of a record album or from that episode of *The Brady Bunch* where Greg tried to be groovy. The woman carried a shoulder bag made from a pair of faded Levi's. The man was carrying a guitar.

"Good morning, Beautiful," the man called out, so I looked behind me to see who he was talking to. No one was there.

"He means you, sweetheart," the woman said.

"Oh."

I had no idea who these people were, but on a perfect planet they'd be related to me somehow.

"Do you know Autumn Evening Schwartz?" she asked.

"Sure. Do you?"

"We're her parents."

This was the other sign of midsummer. The invasion of the parents. But how could these people be Autumn Evening's parents? How could anyone have such cool parents?

"Do you know which bunk she's in?" Autumn Evening's dad asked.

"Same as me. Bunk Two. On the other side of the lake."

Autumn Evening's mom turned to him. "See, I told you. The sign said 'Camp Kin-A-Hurra *for boys*.' Honestly, you'd think we'd never been here before."

"I thought it was an old sign," Mr. Schwartz said in defense. "From before they had girls."

Mrs. Schwartz sighed. "No sense of direction whatsoever."

He was just like my dad. If my dad was a character out of "Yellow Submarine."

"Can't you just drive around the lake?" I suggested.

Autumn Evening's mom explained that they didn't have a car. They'd come by bus. Specifically, a tour bus. Friends of theirs, a folk rock band from New York, were playing a gig in Bangor, so they'd hitched a ride and gotten off at the gate, in order to just drop by. I tried picturing my parents on a tour bus, my mother hygienically covering the seats with toilet paper and my father, whose knowledge of pop music ended around the time Jimmy Durante released "Inka Dinka Doo," off to see America and "just dropping by." It would never happen.

And at my old sleepaway camp it never could happen. In my parents' day, city kids were sent off to camp in an attempt to save them from the scourge of the polio epidemic and outsiders' access was limited. No other children could enter and there was just one day all summer set aside for parents. Long after Jonas Salk came up with his vaccine (and yet another reason for kids to scream in the doctor's office, then be rewarded with lollypops), most camps still held tight to the old rules.

At wretched Camp Cicada, Visiting Day had been even more meticulously controlled than every other day of the summer. On that fateful morning, the Camp Cicada counselors drilled us on what to wear, how to behave, and to mention to our parents repeatedly that we were having loads and loads of fun. The kitchen staff provided box lunches to eat outdoors in a festive picnic style, then, after a rest period during which our parents watched us write them letters, we showed off our skills in various overly supervised athletic events. It was as if we were in a play entitled *This Is What Camp Is Like* and the parents thought we were having a grand old time.

Camp Kin-A-Hurra was a little bit different. With campers and counselors from around the world and no real scheduled activities, Saul encouraged parents to visit whenever they chose. By force of habit, most showed up smack dab in the middle. I was expecting my own parents, once again driving/screaming their way up from New Jersey, to arrive some time before lunch.

"Man, I'm starving. Got anything in that purse?" Mr. Schwartz asked his wife.

Mrs. Schwartz reached into her jeans bag and offered me and her husband Baby Ruth bars. "But if you don't like chocolate," she explained to me, "I've got Red Vines, Abba-Zabas, Bit-O-Honey . . ."

Mrs. Schwartz's entire pants bag was full of junk food. Forget about the folk rock tour bus. It was more likely she'd arrived in a giant, floating Dubble Bubble, the Glinda in my sucrose-coated Oz.

It's the norm for parents to bring candy on Visiting Day. At Camp Cicada the other parents brought shopping bags, even cartons, brimming with goodies and handed over the treats as my mother passed me an open bag of generic Doritos she'd grabbed from a kitchen cabinet on her way to the car. I prayed the nasty girls in my bunk would share with me but that no one would ask me to share with them. And I felt guilty for being angry with my parents for not bringing me more. After all, I was always complaining about my weight. I shouldn't have been eating candy anyway.

The tricky part was that at Camp Cicada it was forbidden to keep food in the bunks. The girls' head counselor threatened that any uneaten treats would be confiscated after the parents left, at the evening bunk inspection. Consequently, campers scrambled to hide their stashes in pillowcases, rolled-up socks, Tampax boxes—anywhere the head counselor might not look. Everyone was well rehearsed, as the search-and-seizure procedure wasn't reserved just for Visiting Day. The Camp Cicada staff regularly checked the contents of incoming mail, insisting packages be opened in front of them, and they took away anything edible. The camp owner claimed the food was returned to the senders, but everyone knew what really happened: the counselors ate it that night.

At Kin-A-Hurra, no one cared if there was food in the bunks as long as everyone shared it. Over on Girls' Side we were tidy enough to keep our treats stored in trunks. Boys' Side, however, was more like Super Bowl Sunday every day, with bags of chips and cookies scattered across the floor, an open invitation to rodents and vermin. Whenever we dropped by Boys' Side at night, my bunkmate Betty wore a big floppy hat, convinced that if she took it off the bats circling the salamis hanging from the rafters would land on her head and nest in her hair.

"A Baby Ruth would be great," I said. "Thanks."

"Never know when the munchies might hit," she responded as she handed me two. Another morning jog undone.

"I'm waiting for my counselor," I explained. "We ride back on the truck. There's room if you want to ride with us."

"Sure," said Mrs. Schwartz. "We can dig it."

I tried to imagine my parents cruising down the dirt road on the Food and Garbage Truck and had a flashback to my fourth-grade spelling bee, when I won by correctly sounding out "preposterous."

By the time Maddy finally emerged from Jacques's office, the truck had already left so we decided to stay on Boys' Side for flag raising and breakfast. Not anticipating early-morning visitors, one of the boys' counselors had declared this day the First Annual Underwear Lineup. Ninety-eight campers and counselors arrived at the flagpole in their tighty whities, surprised to find two representatives from Girls' Side and a set of parents in attendance. It crossed my mind that the boys might think these cool people were my parents and a false sense of pride washed over me until Mr. Schwartz, in a show of solidarity, dropped his own torn jeans. The flags were raised one above the other—American, Canadian, and Israeli—and we sang "O, Canada," because that was where they were in the rotation of anthems.

Feeling a need to hide out, I went into the kitchen and ate with Walter the chef. His pancakes were an entirely different experience when served hot. Now I could understand why Hugh "Huge" Sheveloff was on the famous See Food ("I see food, I eat it") Diet.

"Walter, these are great," I told him. "I wish we could have these every day."

"You just might, my dear," he informed me. "I think Saul must've gotten a fine price on a trainload of flour."

"What does that mean?" I asked.

"Oh, nothing, darlin'," Walter said.

Whenever adults say "Oh, nothing," you know it's something. I peeked out into the dining hall and waved the Fruit of the Loom–clad Philip into the pantry. I figured he'd know the scoop and, as usual, he didn't disappoint.

"You know how it's part of the mystery of Walter that he'll never tell you what the next meal might be?" Philip asked me.

"No," I said. "I never really thought about it. Sometimes when I'm looking at it, I still can't tell what it is."

"Yeah, there's a reason for that," Philip explained. "Walter keeps an inventory. He knows what he wants to buy, what he needs, but Saul insists on doing all the shopping. See, he has this connection in the insurance industry. This guy who insures freight trains and the stuff that's in them . . ."

"What does that have to do with us?"

"Sometimes trains crash," Philip said confidentially.

"So what does that mean?" I asked. "What are you saying?"

What he was saying was that a significant percentage of our meals came from perishable and undeliverable foodstuffs recovered from train wrecks.

"You're making this up!" I shouted.

"Quiet! No one's supposed to know."

"Okay, so let me understand this," I said. "There's a big train wreck and Saul gets a call and he's all excited that people might have been killed because now he can get their soup and salad?"

"That's not exactly what happens," Philip insisted.

"And if supplies are running low and there aren't any wrecks, does he tie some woman to the railroad tracks, like in those old Thomas Edison movies, just to make it happen?"

"See, now you're exaggerating," Philip said, getting all flustered.

"Because it's just stupid. Insurance is for cars and if your house burns down. And—wait—didn't you tell me your father sells insurance?"

Philip cringed. "Shhh. Shhh. There's nothing unethical."

"He's the guy?"

"Shhhhhh!!!"

"Shouldn't that be 'chhh'? As in choo-choo, choo-choo, choo-choo, choo-choo. Woo-woo! Oh no! Look out!"

Philip folded his arms as I mimed a phone call. "Hello? Mr. Selig? Dinner is served."

"Fine," he said. "Go back to Girls' Side. I'll never tell you anything again."

"What? No wait—"

But Philip grunted and walked away, leaving me feeling like I was the one standing around in my underwear.

The four of us arrived back at Girls' Side in time to find Bunk Four's counselor, Cari Lorberfeld, running naked down the aisle between our beds. Her campers had hidden all of her bras and had sworn not to return them unless she streaked through every bunk. As she bounced past us and down the front steps, she nearly gave my mother two black eyes; my parents had arrived.

Seeing my parents standing next to the Schwartzes was like looking at a time line from Mrs. Knoller's Humanities class. My own father still wore 1950s cuffed wool pants and white T-shirts that made him look like Marlon Brando in *A Streetcar Named Desire* and my mother saw no reason to get rid of her mid-'60s plaid elastic-waist pull-ons, the ones she thought were what to wear when she wanted to "look nice." (My parents would continue to wear these clothes, falling more and more out of sync until the end of the century, when they suddenly would be perceived as "retro" and draw compliments.)

My mother stifled a laugh as my father pulled me aside and said, "Don't ever let me catch you running around naked like that girl." Cari Lorberfeld was at least a double-D. Really, it wasn't very likely.

My parents then watched in horror as the Schwartzes presented Autumn Evening with a laundry bag full of candy. Maddy assured them she'd monitor our intake, but we knew she wouldn't. For the first time in my life there was junk food to spare. They also handed Autumn Evening a new blow-dryer and a twenty-dollar bill. "We'll give you some money later," my father quietly told me.

My parents didn't believe in lavishing my brothers and me with gifts, except at Hanukkah. Hanukkah was different. A lot of people probably think Jewish kids grow up envying their non-Jewish friends who have Santa Claus, but I didn't have to because my brothers and I had Mr. Sweeney. A clean-shaven, middle-aged man from New Jersey, Mr. Sweeney occasionally played in my father's Wednesday night poker game and had some sort of job in the toy industry. Every year, he'd invite my parents to his warehouse for a special deal, just for us. Growing up, though, my brothers and I thought he gave out toys to all the Jewish kids—odd since we knew he was Irish Catholic. And my mother taught us revised versions of the holiday classics, titles like "It's Beginning to Look a Lot Like Hanukkah" and "Mr. Sweeney's Comin' to Town."

It was always around Thanksgiving that we'd drive over to Two Guys, the discount department store in Union, New Jersey, to scour the toy aisles, showing my parents what we wanted. A couple of weeks later, Mrs. Fairbanks, a crotchety old neighborhood babysitter who wore snow pants year-round, would come over on that magical night when my mother and father would visit Mr. Sweeney's warehouse. Inevitably, they would discover his inventory was entirely different from that of Two Guys and would toss aside our lists and stock up on whatever he had. As a result, we always got loads of toys for Hanukkah, just never what we wanted, thus creating the unique situation of growing up simultaneously both spoiled and deprived.

I remember one year when I wanted a Midge doll. She had short, reddish hair—kind of like counselor Gita Isak—and I thought she'd be good for my Barbie and Skipper dolls to hang out with. They'd had her at Two Guys, but not at Mr. Sweeney's, so instead my parents got me a Barbie with Growing Hair. I was practically in tears.

"I can't have *two* dolls named Barbie," I tried to explain. "I needed a Midge!"

"You can call her 'Midge,'" my mother suggested.

"I can't call her Midge when her name is Barbie!"

My mother just didn't get it.

"When I was your age," my father broke in, "I didn't have any toys. All I had was a jar of old nickels. And I played with them in the hallway because our apartment was so small."

I must have heard the jar of nickels story a million times yet never once thought to ask my father why he didn't just take his container of coins and use it to go buy some toys.

That same year, my older brother got an elaborate board game called Mousetrap, but it never worked right because we ate some of the pieces.

"So where're you taking me to spend this?" Autumn Evening asked her parents, holding up the twenty. There was only one place. The Schwartzes offered us a day on the town, the town being Skowhegan. The plan was to use the Good Tan Van, which we'd borrowed to get back to Girls' Side.

"Ready to see Skowhegan?" Maddy asked my parents.

"I thought we came to see the camp," my mother answered. "Aren't there activities planned? What do you usually do?"

"Usually it rains," Betty informed her from behind a worn copy of *Go Ask Alice*.

"And when it doesn't," added Dana, "we leave."

"That's Visiting Day?" my father questioned.

"Dad," I tried to explain, "it's not Visiting Day. It's just a day. And you're visiting."

"Maybe you could meet us later for lunch," Mrs. Schwartz suggested. "What was that place with the bread? Flo's?"

Flo's Café, two miles down the road from camp, was noted for its fresh baked goods and recently paroled clientele.

"We'll see," said my father. Which I knew meant "no."

As the van pulled away, my parents asked, "So how's it going? What's new?"

Why oh why do parents ask these questions? It is the unwritten code of adolescence never to say, "We sit around the bunk all day, doing next to nothing except wallowing in self-pity, which you dismiss as 'growing pains,' and obsessing about boys across the lake." I wasn't going to tell them about the prowlers and I had only briefly mentioned the Wolverines' fire in a letter home, prompting my mother to send me my one and only package of the summer, a pair of flame-retardant pajamas that must have been on sale at Rynette's.

"We played softball against another camp," I told them. "I hit a home run and we won."

"So do you like this camp better than the old one?" my mother asked.

This was a question I could answer honestly. "Yes. And I like my counselor a lot, too."

"Dr. Silver did her nose," my mother said.

"What?"

"She had a nose job." My mother just knew it. "Dr. Silver on Madison Avenue. He gives everyone that same little upturned nose. Makes 'em all look like shiksas. You'll go to someone else. Yours will look real. I'm getting some names."

"Have you passed your deepwater test?" my father asked.

"Not really," I said. "It's usually raining."

"It's not raining today," he pointed out.

And that is how I finally managed to swim the twenty laps, with my parents standing on the dock, yelling at me to lift my arms higher, kick my feet harder, and breathe, breathe, breathe, with the Bell & Howell movie camera clacking away.

As I climbed out of the lake and reached for my towel, life-guard Julie Printz congratulated me. "If the sun ever comes out again, you're a deepwater swimmer."

"And doesn't Judy Horowitz's old bathing suit look good on you?" my mother added. Judy was tall and thin and almost as busty as Cari Lorberfeld. It would have fit me better if I'd been wearing it upside down and backwards.

Months later, when we screened the event in the den, my mother got annoyed when she realized I hadn't brought that ratty old pink towel home from camp. I tried to explain that it was among those the townies had stolen off the clothesline. "That towel belonged to my grandmother Celia," she said through gritted teeth. You'd think they'd gotten away with a priceless family heirloom.

"Go get changed and we'll get some lunch," my father said.

"Are we going to Skowhegan to meet the others?" I asked.

"I thought we'd eat here," he said. "Like we did when we dropped you off. Saul took care of us."

"You know that he charges those meals to Mindy's canteen account, right?" Julie asked.

"What?" my mother nearly shrieked.

"Any time you eat here," Julie informed them, "Saul subtracts five dollars a person from the canteen money you gave the office."

We met up with my bunkmates and the Schwartzes at the legendary Flo's, which had once been Eb & Flo's until Eb ran away with a local high school girl, leaving Flo to run it on her own. She didn't have time to write up receipts or ring up bills.

"How much do I owe ya?" the regular customer shouted out.

Flo totaled it up in her head and shouted back, "'Bout three dollahs, Earl. Just leave it in the registah."

He did, along with a big tip on the table.

Walking in as the local man walked out were a serious-looking couple, a man and a woman, overdressed for the occasion, as this was not a court appearance.

"Who are they?" Mrs. Schwartz asked.

A more normal-looking kid walked in behind them. It was Kenny. The Ubers were here. Kenny looked at Dana and Autumn Evening and then he looked at his parents and turned crimson before looking away.

"What are they, feds?" Autumn Evening's father muttered.

"Dad! Shhh!" Autumn Evening pleaded.

Despite my bunkmate's shushing her parents, I ascertained that Kenny's family was loaded, his parents set for life without ever working another day, that they both worked anyway in high-pressure jobs in Manhattan and that they lived in a mansion in Westchester County with horse stables and someone else who scooped up the poop. Even though they reminded me of Haldeman and Ehrlichman, as pictured on the WANTED! poster my brother tacked up on his bedroom door, I was significantly impressed.

When we finished our meal, Flo almost handed Mr. Schwartz the check, then placed it in front of my father instead. I waited nervously to see if he would offer to pay half or just for our family. Thankfully, after looking over the bill and checking the math in his head, my father split the tab with Mr. Schwartz and even bought a loaf of bread for the road.

By late afternoon camp was full of parents, including Hallie's, with her dad in wrinkle-proof Sansa-belt slacks and her mom in mini-check culottes. They brought her a box of Mallomars and a new hairbrush. Dana's parents owned a cracker factory and they placed sample bags of their new Cheesy-O's on every pillow on every bed on Girls' Side. Betty was having a wonderful time with her father, catching frogs in a muddy bog, until someone spoiled their fun by asking what they were doing standing knee-deep in an open cess-pool. All of the parents stayed across the highway at the Oak Pond Motel, most of them choosing it because it was close by, and in my parents' case because of the Triple-A discount.

Saul stunned everyone by offering the girls' parents a free buffet dinner.

"That's nice of him," my mother said.

"Mom," I explained, "we have this every week. It's leftovers. He calls it a 'buffet'. We call it a 'barf-et.'"

It was interesting watching the adults' expressions change as they bit into boiled hot dogs and washed them down with green bug juice. For dessert there was a frosted sheet cake, "From the year gimmel," my mother said, tossing it out after one bite. For once I was glad the food was so bad; it prompted my father to hand over a five-dollar bill, spending money for O'Boyle's.

Borscha's mother turned out to be a classical violinist who'd soloed with the New York Philharmonic. That evening she gave a free concert in the Girls' Social Hall and my mother fixed our per-petually troublesome toilet, getting it to stop running.

"This place seems so unsupervised, so disorganized," I heard her say to Mrs. Bleckman as my mother submerged her hand—diamond ring and all—into our toilet tank. "How many years have you been sending your daughter here?"

"Five," Mrs. Bleckman told her. "And it is a pit, but Dana likes it. And frankly," she said, lowering her voice, "I just want her out of the house. That's *my* vacation."

The night the last of the parents left, it felt good to get our bunk back to ourselves.

"Oh my God," screamed Hallie. "My mother's culottes. I'm so ashamed. I keep begging her to throw those away."

"That's nothing," said Dana. "My parents turned Girls' Side into one big Cheesy-O's commercial."

"I liked your parents," I told her.

"You can have them," groaned Dana. "It's so embarrassing."

It had never crossed my mind before. I wasn't the only one who felt that way.

"And what about the Ubers?" said Hallie. "Did you see them at the restaurant? They're like the Cleavers turned evil."

This was the point at which Autumn Evening burst into tears.

"What?" said Dana. "It's not like you're gonna marry him and they're going to be your in-laws."

"I know that," she sobbed. "He broke up with me today. He thinks he's going on the Allagash and he says he can't be tied down. What the hell is that? I don't even like him. Talk about embarrassing. God, I'll be so glad when camp is over."

But it wasn't over yet and Kenny was free again. If he went on the Allagash trip, however, it would mean he'd be out of camp for ten days and then I'd have ten fewer days to make him like me— or ten more days to think of a way I could make him like me once he got back . . .

Yes, camp was like a tank of gas and now it was a little less than half full. Time to step on it.

to the tune of
"For He's a Jolly Good Fellow"

"The girls went over to Boys' Side
The girls went over to Boys' Side
The girls went over to Boys' Side
To see what they could see"

11

THE LAST THING I EXPECTED WAS TO WATCH TV AT CAMP. ODD, because at home I lived for it. We had two television sets in our house, one in the den and one upstairs. The upstairs TV was a portable, in that it was a twenty-five-inch RCA on a big metal cart that could be wheeled around from room to room, albeit with much difficulty and smacking into doorways. It even had a remote control, although we weren't allowed to use it because, as my mother explained, "If we used it, it might break."

Every kid I knew spent evenings in front of the tube, eager to discuss favorite shows the next day at recess. There were three major networks, PBS, and a bunch of local stations for reruns and cartoons. Movies of the Week were revered as movies. Specials were special. No one had heard of cable yet and Betamax was still just a gleam in some Japanese person's eye. The world was bigger and smaller.

Since we did well in school, my brothers and I were allowed to watch as much TV as we wanted, except for *Hogan's Heroes* (shows about funny Nazis were verboten in our home) and *Dark Shadows* (I have no idea why). I especially loved sitcoms and thought my own family was just like the ones I saw on TV, except we didn't drink milk at dinner, like the goyim. One night my father was absent from the table when my mother set down the food at 5:45.

"Where's Daddy?" asked my baby brother David.

"He's not in this episode," I replied without hesitation.

My older brother Mark's eyes widened. "That's exactly what I was thinking. How did you know?"

I identified with Rhoda Morgenstern, never daring to aspire to Mary Richards heights, and I wanted everyone on TV to be rich. *The Dick Van Dyke Show* was my all-time favorite, but some of the episodes referenced money woes and I didn't want to think that a TV writer had to worry about finances, especially when they lived so modestly in the boring suburbs, like me, and had only one child to put through college.

Due to the Kramdens' dire money situation I never enjoyed *The Honeymooners,* with Ralph's endless string of futile get-rich-quick schemes, and at the extreme end *I Love Lucy* made me physically ill. Though I can appreciate its genius and have seen every episode numerous times, watching it always made me anxious because, despite her best efforts, Lucy never got what she wanted: to be the star in her husband's show. Ricky Ricardo may have loved her, but Lucy never reached her potential because her husband shattered her dreams. What if I got married and that happened to me?

"We're going for a walk," Maddy announced as she entered the bunk after lunch. "You girls need some exercise."

"But it's drizzling out," Betty complained, not that she wouldn't have complained if it were sunny.

"Exactly," Maddy said. "We're going for a walk before it starts pouring. We're going into Canaan to go shopping."

"Shopping." The abracadabra of teenage girls. Suddenly the rain wasn't sounding so oppressive and my bunkmates and I stuffed our wallets into the back pockets of our painter's pants, threw on our ponchos, and headed down the steps. After a pit stop at O'Boyle's, where we loaded up on soda and candy, we headed into town, where we'd no doubt purchase more soda and candy. Hallie kept an eye out for flat nose rocks along the side of the road and Dana started up a chorus of "California Dreamin'."

While I had been dreaming about Kenny day and night, I still hadn't come up with a plan as to how I'd win him over when he came back from the Allagash. Somehow, when he wasn't around, just thinking about him felt like enough and I found myself enjoying my bunkmates' company and doing things like this, this mindless, pointless, endless shopping. But the canoe trip was due back within twenty-four hours and I knew I had to get back on track.

A couple of miles down the road, just as Betty's bellyaching became unbearable, we came upon our destination. "We're here," Maddy announced. "Frank's Fine Antiques."

"This?" we moaned.

No one in the group was particularly excited. I think we all had the same impression of what antique stores sold: big old Victorian furniture, smelly rugs, and unidentifiable brass knickknacks. To our surprise and delight, Frank's Fine Antiques contained nothing fine, nothing antique, and no one named Frank. A stubble-cheeked old buzzard named Buzz sat in a rickety bentwood rocker amid his storeful of absolute junk. There was no organization to the items, no taste, no sense of history, and nothing of real value. It was fabulous.

Most of my bunkmates rifled through boxes of used toys.

"Battling Tops! I used to have this," Dana called out. "And electric football. My brother had that. You'd plug it in and the players just shook. Didn't make any sense."

Hallie found her favorite board game, Mystery Date, and Maddy found a plastic windup chicken that pooped out eggs. Betty found her niche in the used-book section with a worn copy of Sylvia Plath's *The Bell Jar*. Autumn Evening clutched an old black top hat she'd found and communed with its original owner.

"Ah, he was a very important and distinguished man," she said. "Maybe even a president."

I began to doubt Autumn Evening's psychic powers. "I think a lot of regular people used to own those," I told her. "My mother's father had one. He wore it to his wedding."

"Really!" she said excitedly. "Could you imagine what it's worth today? If only you still had it!"

As a matter of fact we did. But how could I tell someone whose opinion mattered to me that my parents were hoarders, that the contents of our house resembled this store, and that my father had all of his clothes from his entire life, which he kept in his closet in chronological order, starting with a pair of corduroy riding pants passed down from his eldest brother?

"So Dad," I once asked, "in the 1920s, poor boys went horseback riding in Jersey City?"

"No," he replied. "We went out to the country. We went to Newark."

Next to the pants hung his U.S. Navy peacoat, pressed against the 1950s garb, adjacent to the starched white shirts from the sixties, and then the polyester era took over. When I questioned my father as to why he kept all this stuff, he said, "Someday my children will be famous and they'll need my clothes for the Schneider Museum."

Not too much pressure on us.

Dana and Autumn Evening came up with the real find: a pair of World War I army helmets, marked down to a dollar each, and I saw something I simply had to have. It was a little glass car, not fragile or dainty but thick and sturdy with highly visible seams. I had no idea why I was drawn to it. It cost three dollars and fifty cents plus tax. If I bought it, it would use up almost all of the money I had left. I was angry I'd seen it because if I hadn't I would never have known what I was missing. It seemed like I was always wanting things I knew I'd be better off without.

As I handed Buzz the money, I felt a sense of satisfaction along with an instant case of buyer's remorse. Hallie noticed the name tag on the inside of my wallet.

"How'd your mom sew that on?" she inquired.

"This one's an iron-on," I explained as we stepped away from the register. "My mother's got ways to label everything."

"Mine's like that, too," Hallie said. "Last year, when I went to Camp Wunzaponna, I stepped in a gopher hole and sprained my ankle, but my mom thought it was a great summer 'cause I came home with all my socks."

"Don't tell my mother," I said. "She'll want to trade us."

Something in a display cabinet caught Hallie's eye. "Hey, Other Mindy, look at this. It's a spoon ring."

A spoon ring is exactly what it sounds like, a ring made from the bent stem of a spoon. In a market saturated with POW bracelets, it was the hot new piece of jewelry for 1974.

Like me, Hallie was from a nerdy family. We were not the hip chicks who hung out at the mall and knew where to buy all the best stuff at all the best prices. She had happened upon this spoon ring by chance and the purchase was now or never. She asked Buzz if she could walk around with it and mull it over.

"Whaddaya think?" she asked, showing it to me.

"I think it's great. I wish I'd seen it first."

My greed and materialism always got the best of me.

"Shoot. It's five dollars," Hallie noted. "Wish I'd brought more money."

Feeling guilty and selfish for my own extravagant purchase, I wanted to find a way to help out. I knew what kids at home with no money did; they stole things. Even kids who did have money stole sometimes and then bragged about it. Even Autumn Evening did it.

"We went to Hawaii last December," my well-traveled bunk-mate had told me.

"Hawaii. Wow. You're so lucky," I said.

"Actually, it wasn't so great. You can't drink at the bar if you're twelve, so I went to the gift shop. There were these little plastic hula dancers with a spring in the middle, to make them kind of wobble up and down."

"Like the kind you'd put on your dashboard?"

"Is that what you do with them?"

"Yeah. Those are cool."

"Okay. I stole one."

I couldn't believe it. "Your parents wouldn't buy it for you?"

"I didn't ask. I just stole it. I just wanted to steal something. Then I think I lost it at the airport."

Autumn Evening didn't know what it was for or why she had stolen it. It didn't sound that hard to do and at least I had a reason. It would be my first ever attempt at shoplifting.

"Hallie, want me to steal it for you?" I asked.

"You could get arrested!" She was horrified. "You can't do that, it's too risky."

But that was what the problem had been all summer. I was never willing to take a risk.

"So you wouldn't steal it?" I asked.

"No," she said. "But if you do, I'll wear it."

Frank's Fine Antiques was located in a barn and there was a second story of trash upstairs in what was once the hayloft. I told

Hallie to come up with me and we milled around a bit and made some noise, pretending to be looking over some ancient Listerine bottles.

"These would look really great filled with colored sand," I said in a loud, obvious voice.

My plan was foolproof. I would take the ring from Hallie and stuff it into the small front watch pocket of my painter's pants, then calmly walk down the steps and out the front door. Buzz wouldn't suspect a thing, as I had already made a purchase. But alas, as I headed toward the staircase, I dropped the ring and it clinked its way down the hayloft steps, landing on the floor at the bottom. I was pretty sure no one had seen it, so I picked up the ring and stuffed it into my pocket, then ran outside as fast as I could with Hallie in tow.

Not two seconds later, Buzz came bolting out and I half-expected him to be toting a rifle, shouting "Git back here, ya varmint!"

"Oh, God, Hallie. He saw me. I'm going to jail."

"You girls know anything about a spoon ring?" he asked calmly.

"Oh, the spoon ring!" I said, revealing the limited acting range of a dancing ear of corn. "I think I left it upstairs."

Hallie's face fell as I turned to run past everyone else—certain they knew of my guilt—and back up to the hayloft where I pretended to look around for where I'd "left" it. Fortunately, Buzz waited downstairs, no doubt suspiciously watching the rest of our group. I came back down a moment later, handed him the ring, and apologized.

On the way back to camp it started to rain. Only Dana and Autumn Evening were protected, as their army helmets shed water well. Dana started up a round of "Ninety-nine Bottles of Beer on the Wall," which Autumn Evening quickly turned into

"Schaeffer Is the One Beer to Have When You're Having More Than One," but I didn't have the heart to fake joining in. I walked back in silence, wondering which was worse: that I'd let down Hallie while discovering I had the potential for a life of crime or that I was awful at doing anything new and out of the ordinary, and therefore my life would never change.

As luck would have it, a group of boys returning from a trip to the bowling alley in Skowhegan spotted us and picked us up in the Green Truck. Maddy thought it might be a good idea to stay on Boys' Side for dinner and stick around for an evening activity. One of the options turned out to be television. TV at camp. That sounded so weird. And what was really weird was that I hadn't missed it at all so far that summer.

A little before nine o'clock, a black-and-white portable was placed on the edge of the stage in the Social Hall and a small crowd gathered around. Someone turned on the news.

"Hey, that's a New York guy," I called out.

"Dan Rather," Philip said as he walked over toward me. "Richard Nixon is about to resign."

"Is anything else on?" Hallie asked.

When the answer was "no," Hallie and almost everyone else left, off to see if Walter had any edible leftovers in the kitchen. I might have left, too, but something about this felt important. I'd slept through the moon landing in 1969 and thought maybe I should stay for this event.

"This is going to be good," Philip said gleefully. "Unless he's got another secret plan up his 'expletive deleted,' Nixon's toast. Too bad they can't turn the White House over to the Democrats. Republicans are evil. Except Abraham Lincoln, but that was a long time ago and he had to pick something quick when the Whigs went out of business."

"He didn't pick the Democrats?"

"Are you a Democrat?" Philip asked, as if he didn't know.

Of course I was. Everyone on my block back home was a Democrat. Almost everyone I knew was a Democrat. Jews especially were Democrats and we loved Hubert Horatio Humphrey, loved him like he was Jewish, too. We thought everyone loved him and then in 1968 he lost to Richard Nixon.

"If kids could vote," my classmates and I lamented, "Hubert Humphrey would have won."

There was only one non-Jewish family in my neighborhood. The Cartenhausers were Catholic and very wealthy, but I think they were still Democrats because they lived in a house that was way too small for a family with seven kids. I envied them; there was always someone to play with and at least every other month one of them was getting a birthday present.

The difference in our religions had come up only once. I was helping Cathy Cartenhauser put on a play about the Bible in her backyard and she tried to convince me that Jesus was the son of God, but I wasn't buying it. When I got home, I said to my mother, "Someday we'll all be dead and when we get to heaven, they'll find out we were right." And that's kind of how the Democratic kids felt about the Republican kids, only we didn't have to wait until we were all dead.

"Least we won't have to hear about Watergate anymore," I said. "I'm so sick of those hearings being on instead of *Match Game*."

"John Dean, Gordon Liddy. They're all going to jail," Philip assured me.

"And what about that guy John Mitchell?" I asked. "The one whose wife wrote *Gone With the Wind*."

"That's Margaret Mitchell," Philip corrected me. "John Mitchell's wife is Martha."

"Oh. Did she write anything?"

"No."

"Well, then, good-bye to her, too."

Our soon-to-be-former president was ready to speak. "Good evening," Richard M. greeted us. "This is the thirty-seventh time I have spoken to you from this office . . ."

I watched and listened for about ten seconds, then realized this speech was about as interesting to me as the rabbi's sermon on Yom Kippur. I wasn't sure if Philip was bored, too, or just so focused he didn't realize his hand was touching mine. I couldn't tell if it was sort of accidentally on purpose and if this was his attempt to try to hold my hand. If I had been a real girlfriend, I would have helped him out and slipped my fingers between his. Instead, I felt I was doing my part just by not pulling away. Strangely, though, I didn't mind that we were touching.

As Nixon continued his heartfelt speech, my mind drifted to what I might be watching if I were at home. Probably a Mets game or reruns of my favorite shows. I was sorry I hadn't been around in the days when most TV programs were made in New York. Nowadays, no matter where my beloved sitcoms supposedly took place, I knew that everyone on TV was really living in Hollywood, that perfect piece of real estate where you never had to shovel snow from the driveway.

Now, most of the shows made in Manhattan were news. News and a couple of cheap local programs, like Officer Joe Bolton who introduced *Little Rascals* shorts on channel 11 and a telethon-length Sunday morning kids' show called *Wonderama,* which ran on channel 5. One time, a kid from my neighborhood appeared on *Wonderama* and made it to the finals of the dance contest. He spent the next five years complaining about losing to a girl.

Richard Nixon was still talking, about some guy "who spends himself in a worthy cause, who at the best knows in the end the triumphs of high achievements and who at the worst, if he fails, at least fails while daring greatly . . ."

I'd completely lost track of what the speech was about, but I noticed a few people around me were teary-eyed as Nixon wished God's grace be with us in all the days ahead. Then, someone turned off the set and we stood and stared at the little circle of light in the middle of the screen as it grew smaller and smaller until it finally vanished.

"Typical politician," Philip remarked. "Do horrible things, mess up the whole country, and then hire some writer to come up with a touchy-feely speech that makes everyone feel bad for you. The guy's a criminal."

Which made me feel better about my own actions. All I did was try to steal a spoon ring and I ended up giving it back. At least I could still say, "I am not a crook."

"Totally manipulative," Philip said with disgust.

"Yeah, manipulating people is wrong," I agreed, nudging closer to Philip when I spotted Kenny at the rear of the Social Hall.

The campers from the Allagash trip were back. Kenny was back. Back in my life. I smiled his way, trying to look casual, but he didn't return the smile. In fact, his face was bright red. Like he'd been crying. Like Nixon's resignation mattered to him. Was that possible? Could it be? My Kenny? Sure, his parents were, but I never would have suspected him, too.

I had only Richard Nixon to thank for giving me *my* secret plan. I knew now how I would make Kenny mine. Starting immediately, I would become a Republican.

to the tune of
"Sugar in the Morning"

"Chicken in the morning
Chicken in the evening
Chicken all noon and night.
Why do we eat chicken?
'Cause Saul's fist is too tight"

12

IF NOTHING ELSE, I FELT BAD FOR PHILIP SELIG.

"Don't you feel like your parents are sort of cheating you?" I asked.

"Out of what?" he wanted to know.

"The whole thing. The party. The presents. The new suit. The chance to spend your summer off, without having to study."

Philip didn't see it my way, that his parents had done him a great disservice when they arranged for him to have his bar mitzvah at camp. To me, it was just plain wrong. Like most of the kids from my Hebrew school class, I'd had a ceremony at the temple followed by a big party. Kids whose parents were rich had the party at the Crystal Plaza. Kids whose parents weren't rich had it at the temple in the big room behind the sliding doors. And kids whose parents were on the cusp of rich, yet sweating out every dollar they spent, had it at the Short Hills. That's where mine was.

"You didn't get to pick out invitations or anything," I argued.

"What were yours like?" Philip asked.

"They were yellow with little green flowers around the edges."

Philip wrinkled his nose. "Flowers? Doesn't seem like you. Sounds girly."

"So? I am a girl," I said indignantly.

"No, I mean I just thought you'd pick something . . . I don't know . . . more . . . or less—" He couldn't find the words.

"Well, you know," I cut in, "my mother picked them out for me."

"So you just okayed them?"

"Not really."

My mother had also picked out the matching response card with boxes to check off if you'd be attending and, if so, whether you wanted chateaubriand or chicken for your main course. She was appalled when two people requested the latter. "Who picks chicken?" she wanted to know. "You're not supposed to pick the chicken. The whole point was to show people we're paying for steak."

This was an important issue for my mother. We'd had chateaubriand at my older brother's bar mitzvah (first time I ever heard of it) and, in years to come, would have it at both of my younger brothers' ceremonies and at my father's synagogue Man-of-the-Year dinner. My mother cultivated a strong relationship with Mr. Trachtenberg, owner of the Short Hills, who referred to every expense as *bupkes*, and she was able to wangle some extra chateaubriand out of him shortly after we got our first dog. My mother found out that the scraps from all the fancy catered dinners were thrown away, so she convinced Mr. T. to have his kitchen staff save them for her and each week she stopped by to pick up the aluminum foil packages. Sheba had steak at every meal while the rest of us continued to dine on hamburgers.

"Who'd you invite to the big shindig?" Philip inquired.

I thought about the two hundred people who'd attended The Day I Became a Woman. "I guess they were mostly my parents' friends and my father's business associates, a lot of lawyers and secretaries. And relatives . . ."

"What about *your* friends?"

"Yeah, they were there."

I still had some friends back then, before spring came and I shocked the town by joining the boys' baseball league, after which I was tacitly shunned. About ten of the kids I'd invited were friends and another ten were kids who'd already invited me to their parties, so I was obligated to invite them back.

"And you had your own kids' section at the back of the catering hall, right?" Philip asked. "With that big, dumb thing of flowers in the middle that all the women fight over at the end for who gets to take it home?"

"No. Only the adults got flowers. We got yellow helium balloons in the middle."

Which made it hard to see each other across the table, a shame since we all looked our best. The girls wore floor-length frilly dresses with multiple rows of tight elastic gathers at the waist and the biggest, puffiest sleeves we could find. The boys were decked out in sports jackets over brightly colored shirts adorned with big clip-on bow ties, the perfect complement to their bell-bottomed plaid pants. Everyone loved crushed velvet.

A lot of the girls wore their first high heels. I opted for heels that were just sort of medium and I was still much taller than any of the boys, obvious when we got up to dance. My parents had hired the Herb Zane Orchestra, a band fond of Glenn Miller tunes and "Alley Cat."

"Right knee, right knee, left knee, left . . ."

Every Jewish kid in Springfield danced exactly alike because we'd all attended the same bar mitzvah dance class, taught by a gym teacher from another town. We learned three dances: the box step, the cha-cha, and a jerky rock 'n' roll move called the horse.

"What else am I missing out on?" Philip wanted to know. I was sorry I'd started this conversation.

"There's the money you get," I reminded him. "All the checks. Like two thousand dollars."

"But the party costs your parents close to three thousand, right? So really, you're losing money on the deal."

This was true. My parents made a point of letting me know that, especially when I asked if I could buy a stereo for my bedroom like all of the other kids' parents let them do, a really good one with a semiautomatic belt-drive turntable and maybe a couple of cool new albums to play on it, like Elton John or John Denver. Anything but those same old Burl Ives records my parents were always buying at Two Guys. But they said, "No, you can keep ten dollars. The rest of the money goes into your college fund."

"I might get to buy a stereo," I said, then felt bad because I figured Philip's parents were even poorer than mine and this camp bar mitzvah was an excuse to save money.

"I already have a stereo," he told me, "and about a hundred albums. But I'm kind of bored with all of them. I'll buy some new ones when we go home."

This camp bar mitzvah thing was starting to look good.

"But doesn't it bother you to have to meet with Saul all summer and practice?"

"We don't really study," Philip said. "Mostly, we sit around and he tells me stories."

"About what?"

"About his life, growing up on the banks of the Mississippi River."

"Saul Rattner? The camp owner? I thought he was from Teaneck."

"He might be a little mixed up," Philip suggested. "I think he might think he's Mark Twain or something. And I'm pretty sure he didn't go to rabbinical school like he told my parents. I'm not even sure he can really read Hebrew. Doesn't matter. I'm ready. I know the whole thing. Wanna hear it?"

For weeks Philip had been asking me to listen to him practice his Torah portion. Anywhere and everywhere, the subject came up.

"Can you listen to me now?" Philip would ask.

"Um, now?" I'd reply. "In the middle of flag raising? While you're in your underwear? Can't you ask Saul to listen?"

And Philip would pout, "I want to know what *you* think."

What I was thinking was that he was six months younger than I was and that girls are supposed to have boyfriends who are older and a couple of inches taller with the potential to make at least twice as much money as we ever would. These were the rules; they didn't describe Philip and I wasn't ready to break them.

"C'mon," he practically begged. "There's no one in the bunk. We could go back there."

"The bunk?"

"We'd have it all to ourselves. We'd be all alone."

All alone? What if he had something else on his mind? And what if he didn't and I really did have to listen to him sing? What if he was awful and I had to plaster a smile on my face and nod and say, "Gee, you're so good"?

"Why don't you surprise me on the big day?" I suggested.

And he did. If I had listened to Philip even once beforehand, I'd have known what an amazing voice he had. Perfect, beautiful and melodic. Something I'd never possess. I wondered why he hadn't auditioned for a lead in *The Sound of Music* instead of just pulling the curtain.

I wasn't the only one who was impressed. Everyone thought Philip was great. Saul was extremely pleased, too, and in an eloquent speech detailing Philip's new duties and what is expected of an honest and humble man, Saul managed to drop in that he was responsible for Philip's training. Then Saul shocked the crowd when he presented Philip with an expensive gift, a magnificent set of fins and snorkel gear, which, throughout the course of his lifetime, Philip would neither use nor ever give away.

It looked like the whole thing was wrapping up and then near-tragedy struck. "Maddy," Saul called out, "won't you please send your girls up here to dance the traditional hora around this young man?" In an instant, the day was no longer about Philip Selig and his induction into manhood; it was about me becoming a public spectacle. Why was I being made to suffer like this? What kind of God would take a gawky thirteen-year-old and make her dance in front of people and Kenny and not be allowed to use any of her two thousand dollars to buy a stereo? And how was it that I was so good at softball and yet so bad at putting one foot in front of the other?

My bunkmates rose and headed toward Philip, but I thought about turning and running off in another direction, to the boys' dining hall where I could hide in the closet under the steps with the rats until it was all over. I thought about it, but I didn't do it. That was the old me who wasn't going to end up with a boyfriend. The new me didn't run. The new me climbed a mountain and would once again rise to the occasion, stride toward Philip—and dance very badly.

"I can't dance," Betty whimpered. Music to my ears if not rhythm to my feet. Surely Betty would look worse than I and all eyes would be fixed on her.

"You dance really well in your sleep," Hallie told her.

"What? I don't dance in my sleep. Why didn't you wake me?"

Autumn Evening had told us, and we believed, that if you wake a sleepwalker she can instantly have a heart attack and die. We let Betty do whatever she wanted in her sleep.

"Just do what I do," Dana advised her. "It'll be over before you know it."

As usual, Dana was right. There was barely enough room for the five of us to circle around Philip. Bumping into one another and trampling over feet, we all looked equally ridiculous. Not that Philip noticed; he was beaming. As the circle broke up and I turned back toward the benches, Philip pulled me aside and asked, "How'd I do?"

"Kinda perfect," I told him, prompting him to spontaneously kiss me on the cheek, which was, when I thought about it later, not horrible.

"Mindy, these are my parents," Philip said, thrusting into my face two short strangers from whom he was cloned.

"Hello," they said.

"Um, hi," I said back.

I was disarmed by the way Mr. and Mrs. Selig looked at me, a look I would become more familiar with in college. A look that said, "You're not much to look at, but you'll be good to my son. Welcome, my future daughter-in-law." A look that, on this day, I did not yet understand.

"Can we get a picture of you two together?" Mr. Selig asked. "Philip's first girlfriend."

But I was not Philip's girlfriend. I was this terrible, awful person using their son because I really wanted to be dating Kenny, who I was hoping was watching so he'd think I was this great person he was missing out on, even though I was really this terrible, awful girl using Philip.

Philip put his arm around me and his father snapped the photo. Or tried to. He couldn't get the thing to work.

I picked Kenny out from the crowd and called to him. "Hey, we could use a little of your expertise!"

"We don't need him," Philip said. "We can do this ourselves."

But Kenny arrived on the scene and showed Mr. Selig what to press as I put my arm around Philip and flashed a great big railroad tracks and rubber bands smile.

"Cheese!"

Next, Philip's parents entered the setup along with Saul, and Kenny captured my act of fraud on film. After the photo op, there was a buffet lunch featuring a choice of falafel or tuna fish sandwiches.

"Thanks for letting them pose with us," Philip whispered. "I know it can be really embarrassing to be seen with my parents." I tried convincing myself it wasn't so bad I was doing this. After all, this was the closest Philip would get to having a girlfriend, so he was getting something out of it. And if it made him look better then it made me look better and then Kenny might be jealous and then we'd all benefit.

"Saul invited us to dinner at his house tonight," Philip said. "What do you think he'll serve? I'm betting on a big bowl of left-over tuna-falafel casserole."

"Unless there's a train wreck with something better on board," I added before biting into my sandwich.

My mouth was still full when Philip's mother asked me if I wanted to join them the next day for Sunday brunch at Flo's. I nodded okay and kept chewing. But about half an hour later, Kenny came over to me and asked if I wanted to go canoeing with him the next morning. "I have something really important I need to ask you," he said.

It could be about only one thing. Obviously, Kenny liked me after all. Maybe he'd liked me all along and dated Autumn Evening first just to work up his nerve. But now, seeing me with Philip and his parents, he finally realized there was no time to spare. He had to make his move. He'd been away for ten days, enough time for Autumn Evening to recover and forget about him and not be mad at me for taking her place. Now he could ask me out.

I couldn't go to brunch with Philip's family. I had to go canoeing with Kenny. But today was Philip's day. Philip's one perfect day. I didn't want to ruin it. I'd wait until Sunday morning to cancel.

"Why can't you go?" Philip wanted to know as his parents sat waiting in their Dodge Dart.

I had an excuse all planned but it wasn't coming out.

"Well, it's just that . . ."

"Is it my parents?" he asked.

"No, of course not," I insisted.

"So then what?" he asked.

"Just . . . something else."

"Kenny?" he questioned, now more angry than hurt.

"Well . . ."

"Okay, fine."

But really it wasn't. I knew it was the wrong thing to do, but when a girl like me has a chance to spend a day—and maybe a lifetime—with a boy like Kenny, there really is no other choice to make. It's like chicken or chateaubriand.

". . . The boys we call our own
will wear glasses and braces and smell of b.o. . . ."

13

Long before Freddy Krueger, *Friday the 13th,* and the onslaught of low-budget slasher flicks, there was the original story of murder and mayhem, the legend of the Cropsy Maniac. Story goes that Cropsy was just your average Joe until he was tragically disfigured in a fire, a fire started by kids at camp. Sporting a hook for a hand and hate in his heart, Cropsy was bent on revenge, waiting at night in the dark of the woods, waiting for campers to cross his path, waiting for a chance to capture and kill them. And, coincidentally, whatever camp you were at when you heard this tale, well, my friend, that was the one where Cropsy lay waiting.

Unless you went to Camp Kin-A-Hurra. We didn't believe in the Cropsy Maniac because we didn't need made-up stories about a homicidal madman; we had the real thing. This was not the stuff of urban legend; it was the stuff of rural reality. Just two summers earlier, in August of 1972, a sixteen-year-old girl from the town of Hinckley had been hired on to help out at the stables. When she disappeared at the end of her first day, everyone assumed she didn't like the job and had decided not to come back. In truth, she had never left.

Horseback riding was never particularly popular at Kin-A-Hurra. For campers, it meant wearing heavy corduroy pants and helmets in the rain, and for the saggy-backed, ancient horses Saul rented for the summer, it meant having to move. Consequently, the two groups of mammals tended to leave each other alone. But a few days after the girl's disappearance, the horses were extremely active, running around erratically, whinnying, spooked.

Sixty-year-old Amanda Bernhardt, a retired rodeo performer who ran the stables, discovered the reason when she spotted the sixteen-year-old girl's hand sticking up from the mud by the water's edge. At first, all of the male foreign counselors were under suspicion— because they were male and because they were foreign—but the killer turned out to be a local man, the girl's jealous ex-boyfriend.

I knew this was a true story because Autumn Evening had photos of the police and FBI taping off the area. To her disappointment, they wouldn't let her get closer to question the hovering soul of the lifeless body. Today was the second anniversary of the murder and this was the romantic spot on the lake Kenny had chosen for our rendezvous.

"Nothing ever happens at this stupid camp," Kenny complained as he stared at the sky while I slapped at mosquitoes landing on my feet and arms, since I'd forgotten to spray on Off. "Have you ever been more bored in your life?"

I thought back on the summer so far: the bunk burning down, the prowlers breaking in, Mindy Plotke falling from the mountain, and the miniature golf excursion that ended in carbon monoxide poisoning.

"You're right," I said. "Nothing much happens here. But at least Nixon got to end the war before he had to leave office."

Kenny looked at me. "Nixon?"

I needed to sound like an informed Republican. This was my chance to show off for him. I needed to summon up my full knowledge of current events.

"I heard Henry Kissinger is Jewish."

"Are you a Republican or something?" he asked.

"Aren't you?"

"Me?" Kenny shouted. "I hate the Republicans. My parents are Republicans. I am not a Republican."

"Then how come you were crying when Nixon resigned?"

"I wasn't crying," he shouted defensively. "I was just mad. And it had nothing to do with Nixon. The back of my camera opened up and the film fell out. All of my Allagash pictures? Gone."

Kenny reddened again at the memory.

"Couldn't other people make copies of theirs and mail them to you?" I asked. "They wouldn't be exactly the same, but—"

"I want my own!" he yelled.

"Well, maybe you could go again next year and take some more."

"I don't think I'm coming back," Kenny muttered, pushing off the shore and paddling a short way back into the lake.

I panicked. "Where would you go?"

I couldn't lose track of him. I needed to know where he'd be.

"Maybe I'll go to some other camp."

I knew this was ridiculous. The names scrawled on the walls and painted high on the rafters made it clear that this almost never happened. All of the North American–born campers returned year after year to Kin-A-Hurra with only a couple of exceptions, when their parents insisted they have other experiences. This usually meant a summer picking fruit on a kibbutz in Israel or six weeks on a bus traveling cross-country with a temple group. Summer school if you really screwed up; Hawaii if you were good. No one from Kin-A-Hurra ever signed on for Outward Bound. It would have been redundant.

"Didn't you think Saul's house was really nice?" I asked. I needed to change the subject. "You're so lucky you got to see it."

"I got to see it 'cause I was kind of unconscious."

"Oh. Yeah. So I guess you don't remember."

"I've been in it before. It's like a house. I don't know. Like the one my family has in the Poconos."

"I thought you lived in Westchester County."

"We have a vacation house in the Poconos. For skiing."

Skiing. Now there was a sport I had no interest in. So much clothing. So much equipment. So much snow.

"I'd love to learn to ski," I said.

"That's nice. Look, here's the thing I need to ask you about."

I gave him my full attention. "Uh-huh."

"Autumn Evening and I broke up before the Allagash, so I'm not going with anybody now."

This was it. Kenny was going to ask me out. Even if he didn't come back to camp, he'd be mine for the rest of this summer. My fairy godmother was tapping me on the head. I could feel the magic wand.

"So," he said slowly, "think I should ask Hallie to the Banquet Social? She's not exactly my first choice or my second choice or my third, but there's nobody good—"

I didn't hear the rest of what he was saying because when you're a balloon that's deflating, wanting to fly about willy-nilly, smacking into walls and making obscene noises before crashing to the ground, lifeless and dead, it takes everything in you to sit still in a boat.

"Has she ever said anything about me?" he asked.

She'd said he was a jerk a bunch of times. Every time she told me I should like Philip.

"I don't think that's a good idea," I mumbled.

Kenny thought about it a moment. "Hmm, might make me look desperate."

"That's not what—"

"You and Phil are pretty lucky," he said. "You're a good match. You're both—different."

"What's that supposed to mean?" I asked, even though I knew what he meant.

"Just different from the others, somehow. Just, you know, different."

How could Kenny know what I was different from when he hardly knew me at all?

"You belong together," he said. "You're lucky."

But I wasn't feeling lucky. On behalf of Philip, and myself, I was feeling insulted. And then, surprisingly empowered by the insult.

I'm not exactly sure at what point I'd stood up, but I was towering over Kenny now and looking down at him. Looking down and really, truly wondering what it was I had liked about him, what I had liked so much for so long. Maybe it was because I looked menacing or maybe it was just the humidity, but a single bead of sweat was dripping slowly down the middle of his nose.

"Why don't you have a seat?" Kenny suggested.

"Why?"

"'Cause you're gonna tip us over. C'mon, sit down!" he yelled.

But like always I just froze. And I stood there watching that bead of sweat as it made its way down his beautiful nose. His flawless nose. His perfect, perfect nose.

I thought I had adored Kenny for his many good qualities, his affinity for the outdoors, his natural leadership skills. All the things I didn't possess. Alas, I was as shallow as the ice cream dishes at Howard Johnson's. Staring down at him, really studying him, it finally hit me. Kenny was not what he appeared to be. Or maybe he was exactly what he appeared to be and I had failed to notice it. I knew now that I had loved him for one reason alone; it was as plain as the nose on his face. And it wasn't even that I wanted him for his nose, I just wanted that nose for me.

"What are you staring at?" he yelled. "Sit down!"

"Maybe I should tip us over," I suggested.

"Are you nuts?"

"They say it's good to try new things. Maybe it'll give you one interesting story to tell about this summer," I suggested, leaning toward the side and rocking the boat.

"Cut it out!" he yelled, worried I might actually try to overturn us.

Which I wasn't really planning to do, but I also wasn't planning on Kenny pulling out a paddle and using it to push me back. And I really wasn't planning on tripping over the paddle and falling overboard. Alone.

"Happy now? Was this a good new thing to try?"

No. It was a very bad idea, one of many bad ideas I'd had this summer, on a par with our government's attempt to get us to switch over to the metric system. And now I was in the water, in the dirty smelly water. We hadn't brought life jackets and I was still, at best, a lousy swimmer and being in my clothes made it even harder.

"Um, could you help me get back in?" I gulped.

"No way," Kenny snickered.

"You want me to drown?"

"Are you that bad a swimmer?" he asked. "You're gonna drown in three feet of water?"

I put my feet down and stood up. The water came to my waist.

"Oh. It's not deep. It's just kind of muddy at the bottom."

"That's not all mud," Kenny corrected me.

"Then what—?"

"Ask the horses," he sneered. "And you're not bringing that into this canoe."

Kenny began paddling away, then stopped.

"Um, you're not going to mention this to Hallie, are you?"

No. I was not. I was not going to tell her how hard I'd worked to be rejected. I was going to sneak back to Girls' Side and throw my "muddy" clothes into the shower, in an attempt to wash away the memory of this day.

The only way back was on foot. Wet and dirty and yet, at last, relieved. As I played back the Kenny debacle in my mind, a stinging sensation went through me, but not one of realization; it was a literal, real live stinging sensation. I was surrounded by a swarm of bees, but these were not the usual friendly bees we passed through every Saturday morning on the way to Boys' Side. I was in a different place now, one I'd never given much consideration before, and I was standing on a beehive that must have fallen from a tree.

"Yow!" I screamed as I smacked at the assailants and tried to run, but they were faster than I was.

"Stand still!" I heard someone yell.

A girl about my age was standing on the front steps of one of the cottages along the Public Beach.

"Stand still and they'll go away."

I did as I was told and within a minute the bees were gone. Perhaps down the road to visit their cousins.

"Did you get stung?" the girl asked.

"I think just one on my arm," I told her.

"Wanna come in and put some baking soda on it? Won't hurt as much."

I knew the rules about talking to strangers. I wasn't sure if a townie my age along the Public Beach counted.

"I'm kind of dirty," I said. "Muddy."

"You could stand in the doorway," she said.

This seemed safe enough and gave me the opportunity to glance around inside the home. I'd assumed that all hicks were stupid or crazy and that they lived in substandard housing filled with items stolen from our clotheslines. This house, however, was pleasant and cozy with lots of gingham fabrics. A whole lot nicer than our accommodations and this girl was a whole lot nicer than Kenny. I guess there were a lot of things I'd failed to notice so far that summer, a lot of things that were right in front of my nose.

I thanked her for the wet paper towels and baking soda without asking her name or giving her mine.

"See ya!" she called out as I headed back down the steps.

"Oh, yeah," I said. "See ya."

We could have been friends now, or at least friendly, but we both knew it never would have lasted.

What would last was my dislike of Kenny. I saw him now for what he was and, finally, I saw Philip for what he was, too: a nice boy who liked me, who, come to think of it, I liked back. There was only one week left of camp. Could Philip ever forgive me?

I managed to sneak back onto Girls' Side unseen, where I showered and dressed and planned my next move. When I saw him the next day, I would ask Philip to the Banquet Social. Nothing was going to get in my way.

Little did I know war was about to break out.

to the tune of the Dr Pepper
"I'm a Pepper, You're a Pepper" jingle

"I go to Kin-A-Hurra and I'm proud
I'm part of a very special crowd
And if you look around these days
There seems to be a very special craze
Oh! I am special, he is special,
She is special, we are special
Wouldn't you like to be special, too?
Be special, come to Kin-A-Hurra,
Be special, come to Kin-A-Hurra . . ."

1 4

SUNDAY NIGHTS WERE SLOW AT CAMP, A GOOD NIGHT TO SIT ON YOUR bed and listen to the rain, the rain that I hoped was washing the last of the horse manure off of the pants I'd hung on the line.

"Mail call!" Maddy announced, entering the bunk with a stack of letters and a package.

"But it's Sunday," Betty pointed out, referencing a calendar and her forty-nine black marks on the wall. "There's no mail on Sunday."

"There is if the office forgot to drop it off yesterday," Maddy said, handing the package to Dana, who immediately tore it open.

"Yes! Thank you, Mom!" Dana announced. "Makeup for the Banquet Social!"

Makeup? We were supposed to wear makeup to the Banquet Social? I couldn't go the way I looked? I didn't have any makeup. I didn't even know how to wear makeup. The only time I ever wore it was in second grade when a girl in another class moved to Connecticut a week before their play. I got asked to take over her role as the queen in *The Chinese Sleeping Beauty* and their teacher, Mrs. Schumann, needed to make my eyes look slanty. Forget asking Philip. I'd have to stay back in the bunk. Maybe in the closet, hunched down by the shoes.

"Letter for you, Mindy," Maddy said, passing me a lime green envelope sealed with colored wax and Wacky Pack stickers. It was from Shelly Landau, a classmate of mine since fourth grade. It's not that we were good friends or spent time at each other's houses after school, but when you are away you need to get mail. I'd heard that Shelly was good at writing back, so we'd swapped addresses. Shelly was spending the summer at Camp Marvin Berman in the Catskill Mountains. Camp Marvin Berman was a fat camp. According to her letter, she'd lost sixteen pounds so far. By my calculation, this meant that Shelly, who was exactly my height, now weighed less than I did. And was probably wearing makeup.

Most of the letter was about Color War. A staple of camps across the nation, Color War is the summer camp equivalent of the Olympics, in which campers and staff split into two teams and face off in a series of sporting events. The ultimate challenge to one's athletic prowess and sense of competition, Color War can last anywhere from three days to more than a week. The name is a throwback to the old days, when every camp had two official colors and campers wore one or the other to represent their teams. Apart from awful places like Morningside/Morningwood, hardly anyone wore their camp colors anymore except when it came time for Color War.

Though the event generally took place somewhere in the second half of the summer, the tradition was to keep the official start date hush-hush from everyone except the staff members in charge, who temporarily became generals and lieutenants. For the rest of us, it was as if Color War were some sort of Pearl Harbor–like surprise attack and you had to break from your usual routine to answer the call to arms. Shelly wrote to me that Marvin Berman, owner and director of Camp Marvin Berman, spent a lot of money on an elaborate "breakout" scenario, hiring a pilot with a small plane to fly overhead and drop multicolored leaflets detailing who was on what team and in which events each camper would compete.

When I was eleven and went off to Camp Cicada, I was under the impression that the goal of camp was to provide a perfect world, a land of fulfillment, the kind of place that would make the rest of your life pale by comparison. Camp Cicada did not meet my expectations, but I did like Color War. The one disappointing thing Saul told me when he came to our house was, "We don't stress competition. You'll make lifelong friendships. And maybe a potholder or two." He said his camp didn't have Color War. And I believed him, until that Monday morning.

No leaflet-filled plane flew overhead, but we did see two male counselors, one dressed in a blue sweat suit, the other in a red one (our unofficial official colors), take off on water skis from the Girls' Side dock and head across the lake toward the boys' dining hall.

"Color War!" several girls called out.

"I don't understand," I said to Dana. "Saul told me we don't have Color War."

"You haven't caught on yet?" she asked.

The tales of nonexistent fruit carts and paneled, heated bunks should have been a clue. Saul Rattner was a man with a plan, a plan to sell you on his camp no matter what it took. When Saul met a prospective camper and his or her family, he'd look the kid over and try to figure out what they wanted and then tell them he had it. Or, in my case, didn't have it. Spotting a chunky girl who bit her nails, Saul assumed I was worthless on the playing field, just another potato sack of mediocrity to toss aboard his "cartload of Mindys," and not a girl who, in actuality, had won the coveted President's Physical Fitness Award in gym class and now possessed a framed certificate stamped with a replica of Richard Nixon's signature.

"So he was lying?" I asked Dana.

Not exactly. Just as the sweat-suited boys' counselors reached their shore, our three waitresses ran out of the kitchen, banging pots and pans together and screaming. When they turned around, we saw that they were naked under their white aprons and had words written in red and blue Magic Markers across their rear ends. Standing cheek to cheek, their three tushies spelled out "Kin And Hurra," and so began a day-and-a-half event Saul called Kin and Hurra. Not exactly Color War, not exactly *not* Color War.

Campers buzzed with excitement as Wendy Katz stood up to read off the team rosters and I thanked God I wasn't a waitress and didn't have to run around like that. I was on the Kin team, red shirts for us, which was fine since Judy Horowitz had handed down a few. Some girls, wearing the wrong colors, dove under the tables and traded with each other as we broke into two groups, on opposite sides of the dining room, to practice team cheers. The two favorites were "Win Kin!" and "Nothing rhymes with Hurra, hey!" and then we were trucked over to Boys' Side—the center of the universe—to let the games begin.

I crossed my fingers that I'd be on Philip's team. It'd be fate. We'd win this thing together. Jumping off the back of the truck, I looked around for the boy I should have been dating. There he was—in a blue shirt with a blue bandanna tied to his blue denim shorts.

"Good thing your Mets cap matches," I called out and waved.

"Nothing rhymes with Hurra, hey!" he shouted at me and turned away.

Philip was now my enemy.

Ordinarily, Color War is heavy on sporting events, both on the field and in the water. Strengths in running, swimming, and boating are widely celebrated. The Kin and Hurra version was a little bit different. Here, the emphasis was on concocting events in which everyone could compete.

Upper camp, those twelve and over, started with events on land while the lower camp went down to the waterfront. Betty, chosen to be our captain, which had to be a mistake, was wild with power.

"You can win the girls' softball throw, right?" she asked me. "Right? Right? Tell me you can do it! Tell me! Tell me! Tell me!"

I liked her better when she was reading.

As Betty annoyingly screeched "Win Kin!" I threw the ball twice as far as any of the other girls. Following that, I helped my team to victory in newcomb, a game that's a lot like volleyball except that you're allowed to catch it, and then we ran some co-ed relay races around the benches down by the Torah tree.

For those who couldn't run faster, jump higher, hit the ball harder, or otherwise fulfill the Wonder Bread promise, there were separate events. I sat on the sidelines watching some of these campers peel the shells off hard-boiled eggs, points awarded for style and speed. Following this contest, equally spastic brainiacs reassembled the shells via mathematical calculations, in these, the days before computer camp.

Before the next round of competition, there was lunch, which all two hundred or so of us ate together in the boys' dining hall, as if things were normal and we weren't divided. As if we would all be friends again once the battle was over. As if you could turn it on and off. As if Color War wasn't really important, just an academic exercise, some grand opera parody of what life would be like at some other camp.

After the meal, we split into our teams again. We had only a few hours to put together Creativity Night, to be held on Girls' Side in our beautiful and greatly underused Social Hall, located in the woods atop a steep hill. The event turned out to be little more than an excuse to make up skits ridiculing Saul. "Our team," General Lars Snorth announced, "the Kin team, will make a show called

Rattner Boulevard. Okay, so what is it?" People jumped in with ideas about stores that sold cesspool deodorizers, carbon monoxide detectors, and a lifetime supply of rain ponchos. There was a traffic light on the boulevard that never worked so all of the cars and people continually crashed into each other and the injured were taken to the hospital via the Food and Garbage Truck. I was assigned a role as one of the talking birds in Rattner's Pet Shop. When customers entered, we shouted out, "Cheap! Cheap! Cheap!"

Remarkably, in spite of all of the day's events, Creativity Night ended with both teams in a dead heat. Tomorrow, we'd be starting out fresh. Kins and Hurras alike, we rose as one group to sing "Taps" before the boys climbed into the Green Truck for the ride back to their side of the lake. Those with significant others, regardless of team affiliation, made brief detours for a goodnight kiss before boarding.

As we stood watching the truck pull away into the darkness, I wasn't thinking about Philip. I had a bigger concern. *If only it would rain* . . . Because unless I lost fifteen pounds in my sleep I was going to be a big-nosed blob in a bathing suit dog-paddling my way through the next day's waterfront races.

I was so desperate to be excused from the waterfront events that I ate a banana the next morning for breakfast. It didn't succeed in making me violently ill, as I'd hoped, but General Gita Isak knew something was wrong.

"Are you sick?" she asked. "'Cause that's going to be really unpleasant if you upchuck on the truck."

"Not that sick," I said. "Not really. I'm just not a good swimmer."

I think she caught my drift because I found myself in three contests, all of which kept me from getting completely wet and allowed me to keep my shorts and T-shirt on over my bathing suit. My most successful event was the Girls' Watermelon Heave, which was really pretty similar to the softball throw, only this time hurl-ing large fruit into the lake.

I was surprised to see Kenny and Philip among the contestants in the boys' solo canoe race. Kenny, a Kin, would undoubtedly beat Philip, but he could still lose to Eric Lorberfeld, counselor Cari Lorberfeld's younger brother, also fresh from the Allagash. It was odd these two whitewater veterans had entered the race. It seemed so unnaturally un-Kin-A-Hurra-ly competitive. Come to think of it, like my own participation in the softball throw. "This is gonna get ugly," I heard El Mosquito groan, and he was right.

The race was not pretty. There were six contestants in all, Kenny and Eric vying to win and the rest just hoping to make it back to shore. Philip and the two other boys had never soloed before and didn't know they needed to alternate sides with their strokes. Each boy paddled on only the right side of his canoe and within a minute there were three boys going around in circles in the middle of the lake in the middle of the race.

Eric, meanwhile, took a quick lead, infuriating Kenny. Kenny paddled hard and fast to catch up, so hard and fast he was unable to stop when he came within inches of Eric. "Win Kin! Win Kin" turned into shouts of "Look out!" and "Watchit!" as Kenny crashed his canoe into Eric's, sending them both into the side of the dock and out of the race. Philip, now moving his paddle to the left side of his canoe and back again, and taking a cue from Aesop's tor-toise, easily glided to shore and took first place. In fact, he took the only place as the other three contestants had to be rescued by motorboat.

The boys' kickboard relay produced an even more startling result. You'd think someone had made a horrible mistake telling twelve-year-old Mikey Schreiber to get ready to jump into the lake. A member of the Hurra team, Mikey would be swimming the final leg of the boys' kickboard relay even though Mikey himself had only one leg.

Mikey was in this situation because Saul did more appalling things than promise golf courses and hydroplanes that didn't exist. P. T. Barnum himself couldn't have done a better job of assuring the parents of prospective campers that Kin-A-Hurra had special facilities for children with special needs, when in actuality we had hardly anything for anyone. Saul referred to these kids as "special campers," but really, they were pretty common around here and what I'd suspected was motivated by little more than pure greed inadvertently paved the way for an avant-garde political correctness.

Mikey stood clutching a blue Styrofoam kickboard with one hand and a teammate, for balance, with the other. Tagged on the foot by a boy in the water, Mikey jumped in, swimming and kicking crookedly toward the rope. "At least the Hurras are way behind," I observed. "Mikey can't be blamed for the loss." And he wasn't. Because Mikey reached the rope first, turned around, swam back—and won. Counselors from both teams lifted him out of the water and carried him in the air, back to the beach where his other leg (the one made out of molded plastic) was lying in the sand, waiting to be strapped back on. Camp owner Saul Rattner was on the beach, too, pipe in hand, a faint smile and an "I-told-you-so" look on his face.

I think some people viewed Saul as the ultimate con man, the lying, scheming owner of a broken-down, worthless mosquito-infested camp who cheated unwitting parents out of their money. Others, meanwhile, saw him as a dedicated and exceptional social worker, a man with the capacity to gather up a campful of outcasts with nowhere else to go and make them all feel like winners, a man who so believed in his own lies that he somehow turned them into reality. And some people, me included now, saw him as a little bit of both.

A friend of mine once described NBA basketball this way: "Give each team a hundred points, put two minutes on the clock—go!" Kin and Hurra was far from over. At the end of the second day, the score was once again tied. It all came down to the last event, the War Canoe Race. Here, the twelve oldest and strongest campers from each team, the ones besides Kenny and Eric who'd survived the Allagash, paddled out slowly to the middle of the lake in the two big old war canoes reserved for this contest. The rest of us—the whole camp—stood on the shore, waiting, until chef Walter Henderson fired off a cap gun and the race began.

"Win Kin! Win Kin!"

"Nothing rhymes with Hurra, hey!"

I had my Instamatic out, snapping photos as the two teams paddled furiously back. It was a close race, both war canoes appearing to hit the beach simultaneously. We would have to wait for the judges (Chef Walter, the camp doctor, and Rhonda Shafter from the theater) to announce the winner over a megaphone.

Five minutes later it was all over. I can still recall the chills that went through me as the winner of the War Canoe Race, and all of Kin and Hurra, was announced, but I cannot for the life of me remember which team it was. What I do remember is that as soon as it was over, everyone on both teams, screaming and hugging, ran into the lake with their clothes on to sing the camp reunification theme, "Chock Full 'O Nuts Is That Heavenly Coffee." Everyone but me again.

I had tried all summer to be like everyone else and what had it gotten me? Kenny? No. Philip? No. Any boyfriend? It had gotten me wet and muddy and embarrassed and sorry I'd tried to change.

Although Camp Kin-A-Hurra's mailing address was Canaan, Maine, a large portion of the camp actually sat within the boundaries of the next town, Skowhegan, a Native American word meaning "a place to watch." This was where I stood now, where I had been all summer long.

My plan was to stay back on the beach, taking pictures, from a distance. That was my plan until my bunkmates saw me, ran out of the water, and chased me down the shore. I figured there was no chance they'd catch me. Autumn Evening was the fastest, having been a Greek decathlete in a former life, but that was a long time ago. We must have looked like we were having fun because other campers began running out of the lake and joining in the race. Ten or so at first and then a couple dozen. "Get her! She's dry!" I heard them yell.

I knew I was in trouble. I was fast but not *that* fast. Sure, I'd won the President's Award, but I was only eighty-sixth percentile in the 400-yard walk-run. I needed an adrenaline rush, like the one in that article I'd read about the grandmother who lifted a car when her grandson got run over on his tricycle. Otherwise someone was going to catch me and then they'd throw me in the lake. With my clothes on. And it'd ruin my camera and my parents would be mad at me and never send me back to camp again. Which might be good, because then I wouldn't have to worry about stuff like this.

No adrenaline rush kicked in and someone had my ankle. And someone else had my other ankle. And when I hit the ground my camera flew out of my hands as two people grabbed my wrists. The trip back down to the lake was swift, kind of scary and kind of fun and kind of like an amusement park ride—the kind you look forward to getting off of. I closed my eyes and held my breath when I knew I was going in, going in with a bigger splat than the big old watermelon I'd hurled a while earlier. From beneath the surface, I could hear the cheers from above.

Everyone was looking at me as I came up for air. It was a moment I knew I'd want to forget but never would because Philip was standing there, right in front of me, snapping a photo—with my camera.

"Camping Out"
by Mindy Schneider, age 13

Oh I love to go a-camping in the great outdoors
Where air is fresh and life is so real.
I love getting up at five in the morning.
I love the disgusting, groggy way that I feel.

I love having four people in a two-man tent
Where you're lucky to sleep for an hour
I love getting up and putting on fresh clothes
When it's been six days since I've taken a shower.

I love the campfire.
The smoke repeatedly stings my eyes.
I love how just when we start the cooking,
Rain pours down from the skies.

I love how we vote to bring the chicken inside the tent.
(I turn out to be the only negative voter.)
I love how hours after there are bones wherever I step
And a wonderful burnt chicken-y odor.

I love the way the clothes are kept.
So neatly—in a clump.
I love baked beans one day, the day after and the next.
I love the oatmeal's every lump.

I love cleaning oatmeal and baked beans off prehistoric mess kits.
It's by far and wide my very favorite chore.
Yes, you can surely tell I'm a great camper.
So adventurous, inventive and so anxious for more.

I love the people who talked me into this camping out caper.
Especially the one who forgot the toilet paper.

But the next time I go camping out,
I'll have everything I need.
I've figured out what it's all about.
I've found a way that's just my speed.

Oh sure, I'll work up to roughing it,
But I've got an easier place where I'll begin.
The next time I go camping out,
It'll be at the closest Holiday Inn.

15

WE WERE NEARING THE END OF THE CAMP SEASON, TIME FOR THE Banquet Social, the big dress-up event on the second-to-last night of camp. In previous years, Boys' Side and Girls' Side had held the banquet part separately, meeting up afterward for the social. This year, Saul's plan was to hold the banquet over on Boys' Side, everyone together, claiming it would promote solidarity, but we suspected it had more to do with a slow week in train wrecks and a shortage of meat.

"How are we all going to fit into the dining hall?" Betty asked. "It was awful during Kin and Hurra. Shoulder to shoulder, elbow to elbow, all squished together."

"That's what was fun about it," said Dana.

"No one will be able to move in their good clothes," Betty argued. "No one will be able to eat."

"Which is exactly what Saul wants," I suggested.

"You're finally getting it," Dana congratulated me. "But we're not going to let that happen."

Dana and Autumn Evening concocted a plan that would not only solve the problem but also give us an excuse for one last middle-of-the-night raid on Boys' Side.

"Rise and shine, everybody," Dana announced at one a.m. "We're going to dine al fresco."

"Sounds good," I said, rolling down my itchy green blanket. "What is it?"

"It's French," said Betty. "Don't you know anything?"

"Yes," I said. "I'm taking French in school."

Which was true, but I'd only learned to conjugate a few irregular verbs so far and I hadn't learned anything useful like "a la carte" or even "ooh-la-la." We just kept reading in our primer about Mademoiselle Simone and her friend Bebe, *l'elephant qui parle.* If I ever went to Paris and met up with a talking baby elephant, I'd know just what to say. Otherwise, I was kind of screwed.

"Al fresco is Italian," Autumn Evening said. "I lived in Italy for a year."

"In one of your past lives?" I asked.

"No, when I was seven. My father taught at a university. I do have a present life, y'know. I'm going to be famous. The dead soul from one of my future lives came back and told me."

"Canoes or walking?" Dana asked.

"I'll take you," Maddy called out, groggy.

"Oops, sorry. Didn't mean to wake you," I apologized. "We almost made it through the whole summer."

"Are you joking?" she asked. "You woke me every night you went out. I never bothered to say anything."

"You're not going to make us jog there, are you?" asked Betty.

"I've been jogging for eight weeks," groaned Maddy. "It's enough already. Let's take the Valiant."

And so it was under a full moon on a crisp August night that we spent three hours removing every single table and bench from the boys' dining hall, and then re-creating the exact floor plan in front of the flagpole on the boys' softball field.

"Voilà," said Dana, as the last moldy old wooden bench was placed under an even moldier old table. "'Voilà', by the way, is French. It means we're done."

"We're done with what?" asked Betty, looking around in astonishment. "What am I doing on Boys' Side? How did we get here?"

"Oh my God, were you asleep this whole time?" Maddy asked.

The rest of us didn't know what to say.

Betty cracked a smile. "You guys are so gullible."

"So you really were awake?" Hallie questioned.

"Duh!"

"Or maybe she was awake before and *now* she's asleep," I added.

"Betty, pinch yourself and show us you're awake," Hallie said. "Or we'll never know for sure."

"Unless we're all dead and Betty is dreaming about us," Autumn Evening suggested. "And then if she wakes up, we'll be gone."

"Okay," I said. "Don't pinch yourself."

"I don't have to pinch myself," Betty insisted. "I'm awake. I'm awake and it's raining."

Which it was.

We ducked under the tables to keep dry, but the rain came right in between the wooden boards.

"Why don't you go hang out with the Foxes?" our counselor suggested.

We waited for the rain to let up a bit first. When it didn't, we made a run for it, through the tables and benches, past the Giant Teepee and the cracked, weed-infested tennis courts. We lost our counselor at the Boys' Side office.

"I'll wait in here," she said.

"Don't you want to come with us?" Hallie asked.

"No. It's okay. I don't want to intrude. Have fun."

Hallie turned to me. "She has the dullest life of anyone I've ever met."

"You think so?" I said. "I'll betcha she's engaged before we all go home."

"Engaged?" shrieked Hallie. "To who? She's not even going out with anyone."

We didn't see Maddy for the rest of the night.

Meanwhile, I was on a mission. If I was going to ask Philip to be my date for the Banquet Social, I was going to have to do it now. I could still change after all. I could become—a girl with a date! Of course, the whole notion of having a date was completely stupid. Everyone was going to the social, whether they wanted to or not. It was understood that this was the one night of the summer you couldn't stay back at the bunk and the one night you could get away with not having a date. So it really didn't matter what he said, and God I hoped he'd say yes.

I thought the idea was to sneak into their bunk, but upon opening the door Dana shouted out, "Ta-dah!"

"Whaddaya want?" Kenny whined, in a tone I now recognized as his usual cranky self.

"We came to warn you it's raining," Dana yelled above the din pounding the tin roof.

"Yeah, that's news. Tell us when it isn't."

He rolled over and went back to sleep without even acknowledging my presence. And I liked it that way.

Everyone knew Dana would be going to the Banquet Social with Aaron Klafter. Autumn Evening was something of a mystery.

"So, like, who ya going with?" Chip Fink asked in a tone that was at once both nonchalant and despairing.

He was taken aback when Autumn Evening answered quickly, "Michael Dushevsky."

The name sounded familiar. I'd seen it painted on a wall somewhere.

"I don't think he's here this summer," I said.

"Of course not," Autumn Evening replied. "He was here for five years, from 1949 to 1953, then he died in an avalanche on a skiing trip in Gstaad. Michael was fifteen. His ghost comes up to camp every summer. I'm going with him."

Everyone stared.

I broke the silence. "There's a place called Gstaad?"

"It's in Switzerland," Autumn Evening explained for the un-enlightened. "Some people don't pronounce the 'G,' but I find that pretentious."

Philip got up and crossed the room, heading for the door. I needed to stop him, to tell him how sorry I was for backing out of breakfast with his parents, for embarrassing him. I'd never wanted to hurt his feelings. I only wanted to do what I thought would make me feel better. He just got caught in the middle of it. I followed him outside to the bunk porch.

"Hey, um . . ." I started.

He stopped and turned. "Yeah?"

"You know, I didn't . . . That thing a few days ago . . . I mean . . ."

"Uh-huh," he said.

"'Cause, y'know . . . I didn't mean to . . ."

"Sure."

"Yeah, well anyway . . . I'm really . . . y'know . . ."

"Okay."

"So you're . . . ?"

"Yeah."

I was glad he understood.

"You going to the Banquet Social?" Philip inquired.

Was it that simple? After all this, was *he* asking *me* to be his date? I needed to let him know I was still available.

"I guess. You?"

"I guess."

Had I made my point? Had he asked me to the social? Did I have my first date?

"Um, I really have to go," Philip added, then turned and ran up the hill toward the bathroom shack.

The rain ended shortly before the wake-up bell and breakfast. We followed the boys down to the flagpole to see the whole camp's reaction to our work.

"Unbelievable."

"It's incredible."

"Never seen anything like it!"

"Everything is so—so clean!"

The waiters toweled off the shiny tables and benches and we dined al fresco.

The break in the rain didn't last long, putting me in a bit of a quandary when it came time to dress for that evening's banquet. I wanted to be like everyone else, to wear my good bat mitzvah dress, purple crushed velvet with scratchy but elegant white lacey trim on the collar and cuffs, but I worried it might get wet. I didn't know what could happen to wet velvet, but I knew what my mother would say: "Why did you have to wear it? Now it's ruined." And even if it wasn't raining, what if I'd gained weight and it was too small on me? If only I hadn't eaten quite so much in the 1960s. I'd be so much thinner now. Why did I never plan ahead?

I went to the back of the closet where no one could watch me and removed the dress from the good plastic hanger my mother had labeled with my name. It slipped on over my head with no ripping sounds, my arms still fit into the sleeves, and the elasticized waist still had some give. For once I was glad I hadn't changed and then I looked down. My ankle-length dress had gotten shorter. Or I had gotten longer.

Peeking through the hangers full of bell-bottoms, hot pants, embroidered denim work shirts, and faux Greek peasant blouses, I looked to see who might be available to help me.

"Dana!" I whispered. "Dana!"

She didn't hear me, but Betty did.

"Dana! Mindy is yelling to you from the closet!"

Everyone came charging in to see what was up. It was obvious. Unless I was going for my younger brother's we-can't-afford-clothing-that-fits-right flood pants look, this dress was a disaster.

"Wow," said Autumn Evening. "It's like a midi. Cool."

"Yeah, and it won't get wet on the bottom, like mine," added Hallie, envy in her eyes.

"You know what you need?" Dana said. "You need me to blow-dry your hair straight."

"Me with straight hair?"

"You don't like the idea?"

"Well, yeah, but I didn't think it was possible. Me with straight hair is like a world where dogs have thumbs and can open kitchen cabinets."

Betty shot an odd look my way. "My brother doesn't have thumbs and he can open kitchen cabinets."

"That's interesting," Autumn Evening noted. "If he comes to camp next summer, Saul can make that an event in Kin and Hurra."

Later, heading down the steps, Hallie leaned in and whispered, "You look great. Too bad you don't have a boyfriend."

"What about Philip?" I asked. "He likes me."

"It doesn't count if you don't like him back and everyone knows you don't."

Well, everyone was wrong. I was wrong. And tonight I was
going to prove it.

With the tables and benches back inside the dining hall, we
sat crowded together, elbow to elbow, all spruced up, except for
the Wolverines, who were slovenly by comparison.

"What's the matter with you boys?" Saul wanted to know. "Is
this some form of protest? The sixties are over. Where are your
nice clothes?"

"They burned in the fire!" a lone Wolverine shouted.

For a moment, Saul was caught off-guard, but then he regained
his composure. "That's no excuse," he said. "You should look nice
tonight. We're having steak."

"Freight train of steak must've crashed," someone muttered.

"Woo-woo!" someone else added.

"No," chimed in Bobby Gurvitz. "It's 'Moo-moo!'"

I just hoped it wouldn't be chateaubriand. I had too many issues with that cut of meat.

As usual, Maddy had abandoned our bunk shortly after our
arrival on Boys' Side, but she did show up toward the end of the
meal. For the first time all summer, Maddy and Jacques entered a
room together. Immediately, the junior counselor girls paddled
their hands against the table and made a dedication: "Quiet, please!
Dedicated to the dining room: 'Maddy Rattner, Maddy Rattner, take
some good advice from me . . .'" But they were too late. Jacques
and Maddy kissed in public for the first time, displaying their af-
fection and the sparkly engagement ring on Maddy's finger.

After the meal came the entertainment. The Chipmunks' counselor, Stuart Goldstein, had declared the theme of the banquet
"Poetry in Motion," which was Stuart's excuse to get up and read
his favorite poem, Lewis Carroll's "Jabberwocky." After that, Betty
read her favorite, the suicide-themed "Resumé" by Dorothy Parker.
And then it was my turn. I was on the program, too.

Word had leaked out that I'd been writing satirical poetry since I was twelve. Tonight, I would make my public debut. I had two reasons to be nervous. First, I'd spilled a tiny drop of gravy on my sleeve, and even if no one in the audience noticed it my mother surely would when I got home, and, more significantly, what if no one laughed at my poem when they were supposed to? And even if they did, there was still that thing again about everyone looking at me, and not just noticing the gravy on my sleeve. Standing on a chair in the middle of the dining hall, at least half the camp would see me in profile. My nose again. That cursed nose.

What if I fall off the chair before I finish and that's the only thing people ever remember about me? Years will go by and campers and counselors will still be telling the tale: "Remember that girl in the purple dress who fell off the chair at the Banquet Social?" But if I did fall off, I could still make the most of it, I told myself. *I could fall on my face and break my nose and then the surgery would be covered by insurance and it wouldn't cost my parents two thousand dollars and I could have it done now instead of waiting until I was sixteen.*

In my mother's last letter she'd told me she found out which doctor did Marlo Thomas's nose. My classmate Kathy Shein had gone to him when we were playing volleyball in gym class and a girl on the other team spiked the ball into her face. That was the doctor my mother wanted for me, the doctor who gave *That Girl* that nose. I wished I were in gym class right now, getting hit in the face with a volleyball. But I was here. At camp. About to recite my poem.

Stuart Goldstein announced me. "Mindy Schneider will re-cite 'Camping Out,' based on her experience earlier this summer at Katahdin."

I climbed up on the chair without falling off and, in that same loud voice that had won me the lead in my second-grade class play, I began: "Oh, I love to go a-camping in the great outdoors, where air is fresh and life is so real . . ."

At the end of the first stanza I got a laugh. Much closer to calm and confident, I recited the rest of the poem and, when I finished, I jumped off the chair to what felt like wild applause. No one seemed to notice the gravy on my sleeve or that I took poetic license, turning the overnight into a six-day trip and mentioning foods like baked beans, which we would have killed to have had in place of peanut butter and peach nectar. *Yes*, I thought to myself, *I think I did okay.*

Such was my triumph that four years later when I applied to thirteen colleges (two I was interested in and eleven safety schools), I attached a copy of the poem along with the required essay. Such was my triumph that when I went back to my bunk's table and sat down, I was aware of a feeling that was at once familiar and foreign, as if I were suddenly transported back to General Swim at Camp Cicada, only this time I wasn't stuck in the Minnow section. I was with the Perch and the Sharks, not winning any races, just in the water. Swimming in the deep water, not afraid I might sink.

The waiters served dessert, a pinkish sheet cake.

"What're those spots all over it?" Betty asked.

"I think they're raisins," said Dana, poking at one. "Or dead flies. Autumn Evening, you know any of these guys?"

When the banquet was over and it was time to sing grace, Saul decided to keep us in the dining hall a little longer, waiting for the rain to let up a bit before we made a dash for the Social Hall. Wendy Katz started up her own dedication and got us singing "Leaving on a Jet Plane," the song that always came at the end of camp.

It was not okay for boys to cry, but many of the girls, especially the older ones, openly sobbed. I wanted to sob, too, though for a different reason than my peers. I would not be leaving on a jet plane. It would be years before I'd go anywhere on a jet plane. I would be leaving in the backseat of a station wagon because my family never had money for fancy transportation. We never had money for fancy anything.

It might have helped if my parents had explained the reason for their frugality, but it wasn't revealed until years later. I have a master's degree, Jay has a master's and a PhD, and Mark and David each went to law school. All told, the four of us have amassed some thirty-two years of higher education at private universities and upon graduation not one of us owed a penny. That was where the money went. But as kids we just thought we were poor.

"I liked your poem," I heard someone behind me say.

It was Philip again. Good old Philip.

"Thanks."

"Um . . . so you're going to the social, right?" he asked.

Saul was standing in the middle of the dining hall, calling for silence. He'd stepped out to take a phone call and learned that the rain was not expected to let up any time soon. Rather, it was likely to develop into a hurricane, one that might wash away all of camp. We still had thirty-six hours left, but we would not be spending them here. We were fleeing to higher ground. I turned to Philip to answer his question, as to whether I'd be attending the social: "I'm thinking I'll skip it this year."

to the tune of
"Rise and Shine"

"The Lord said to Saul
There's gonna be a flood-y flood-y
Lord said to Saul
There's gonna be a flood-y flood-y
Get those children
Out of the muddy muddy
Suckers of Camp Kin-A-Hurra

So rise and shine
And give Saul your money, honey
Rise and shine
And give Saul your money, honey
Rise and shine and
Give Saul your money, honey
Suckers of Camp Kin-A-Hurra

So Saul, he built them
He built them a bunk-y bunk-y
Saul, he built them
He built them a bunk-y bunk-y
Made it out of
Junky junky junky
Suckers of Camp Kin-A-Hurra"

16

Autumn Evening held up two outfits. "Which pajama ensemble should I wear?" she inquired. The boys had seen us in our nice clothes; now we had to determine what they'd see us in next. Autumn Evening decided to go with the man-tailored silk jacket and lounge pants. "It's all about style, dahling," she told us, glamorously pretending to smoke an incense stick, while I placed my purple velvet party frock back on its hanger, relieved not to be playing dress-up any more. If Philip was going to like me, he was going to like me in gray sweats and a rain poncho.

Taking only our sleeping bags, pillows, a change of underwear, and secret stashes of food (and my toothbrush—always my toothbrush), we bade farewell to our camp in record time via every available vehicle. "If the rest of our stuff gets washed away," I asked Maddy, "do you think Saul could write me a note for my mother? Otherwise she'll think I lost everything." I considered bringing along my clarinet. Not to play it, just to keep it dry.

The boys had taken the Green Truck, leaving us only the Good Tan Van and the Valiant, so our counselors crammed girls into their old clunker cars and the kitchen staff rode on the Food and Garbage Truck. Saul let a couple of special campers ride along in his jeep. Our destination: the Skowhegan Junior High gym.

The boys had already arrived and laid out their sleeping bags on the far side of the basketball court. The girls were about to unroll theirs as well, when it was announced that the social would go on as planned. Jacques had dragged along a ham radio in order to spend the night monitoring weather reports, but Wendy had grabbed an old phonograph and a handful of records. Thanks to her, we'd be dancing the night away to the Jackson Five, the Spinners, and Jefferson Airplane.

All of the cool kids, the go-with-the-flow types you knew would be successful adults, took to the floor. Girls were dancing with girls and even some boys joined in. Others on the sidelines (literally, since we were on a basketball court) clapped and swayed to the music. I'd been aware of two basic kinds of kids at Kin-A-Hurra. The first were the Legacies, mostly children of former campers. Rich kids destined to lead relatively easy and productive lives, they seemed to possess no insecurities or feel a need to judge and belittle the other group. Then there was the other group, the Losers, the paste-eaters Saul conned into coming to this place in spite of their unbridled self-doubt and absolute lack of social skills. This was who our camp was: Legacies and Losers, but put us all together in one room in our pajamas and we kind of looked the same.

"Um, wanna dance?" Philip asked as Michael Jackson's "I Want You Back" blared from the mono speaker.

Something totally unexpected happened as I struggled to remember the horse. It's not that I suddenly became Ginger Rogers. It was something far better: Philip couldn't dance at all. Arms and legs flailing every which way, I had to duck a couple of times not to get hit. And the best part was, he didn't seem to care. When the song ended, someone changed the record, putting on a 45 of Diana Ross's "Touch Me in the Morning."

Philip looked at me and shrugged. "You wanna?"

Now I knew why I had learned the box step. Standing at least four inches taller than Philip, I bent my knees and hunched down as much as I could without looking like I suffered from an early onset of osteoporosis and placed my hands over his shoulders. He placed his hands on my waist, though not too tightly, as if he was nervous or something. And then we were doing it. Dancing. Slow dancing and touching. It was so effortless, so easy, and, to my disappointment, so totally boring. We stepped back and across and up and across and back and across again, until my knees hurt and my back itched, right in that spot in the middle that's so hard to reach. Philip sensed something wasn't right.

"Should we go outside?"

"Isn't there a hurricane?"

But if I'd said no, we'd have had to stay inside and dance some more and I was getting a charley horse in my right leg.

Philip took my hand and I hoped he wouldn't notice that I bit my nails, a bad habit I intended to give up when I got to high school. Philip's hand was kind of sweaty and clammy. He looked at me funny and then I thought he was going to try to kiss me again. A real kiss this time, not a fake dying from carbon monoxide–induced kiss. The kind where we'd both knowingly participate.

Unlike the girls in that Judy Blume book, *Are You There God? It's Me, Margaret*, I had never practiced kissing on my pillow, or anywhere else for that matter, though I had tried to research the topic. My father never had much time for pleasure reading, but this didn't stop him from joining numerous book clubs and buying dozens of cut-rate volumes a year. One of his purchases was a set of four thin books called *The Life Cycle Library for Young People*. Sometimes I'd sneak into the study at the back of our house and read the chapters about dating. Mostly the books had tips for boys, offering pointers like "before asking a girl out, consult your wallet," but nothing about what to do the first time you kissed and where anything was supposed to go.

I'd tried to talk to my mother about dating, but somehow the conversations were more about her than about me. She'd always go back to the time when she was twelve and Boris Kazikoff got fresh in the middle of *Going My Way*. But all I knew was that she didn't kiss him.

So when exactly was her first time? How did she know? How does anyone know and why didn't she tell me? Was it her way of saying that kissing wasn't for me, would never be for me, and, if so, why not? And how come two Jewish kids in Brooklyn went to see a movie about a priest? Why couldn't I ask and have answers to the questions that mattered?

We were standing in the doorway. It looked like Philip was about to say something or do something. Nothing my mother ever told me popped into my head. My father had certainly never broached the subject either, never given me advice. Well, he'd given me advice but not anything pertinent.

One time when I was four years old, we walked over to the high school and watched a football game through the fence. When my father found out that admission was free after the first half, he took me in and I got my first glimpse of a marching band and those girls with the amazing pom-poms. Watching me watching them intently, my father leaned over and warned, "Don't ever be a cheerleader." I grew up thinking those girls were evil. Eventually, when I was about thirty-five, I asked him why he'd said that to me, expecting the answer to contain the wisdom of the ages. He thought about it a moment, then remarked, "I said that? Huh. I have no idea." I can only assume he was seeking to protect me, to keep me focused on academic pursuits, to save me from becoming just a sex symbol. Not to worry.

Philip showed me a pack of Marlboros hidden in his front pants pocket. "You smoke?"

I remembered the answer Hymie the Robot on *Get Smart* gave: "Only when I'm on fire."

Philip laughed. "I love that episode."

We had most certainly grown up watching all of the same shows.

"Okay, sure," I said. "I'll have one. I've always liked the smell of cigarettes."

Philip was surprised. "Yeah? A lot of people don't."

"Well," I explained, "I like how they smell before they're lit. Sometimes at Hebrew school we'd go into the girls' room and take them apart and smell them."

He looked at me like that was a peculiar remark.

"I guess it was just something to do," I said.

"You want to do that now?" he asked. "Just stand here and shred them?"

That would have been my preference, but I had to say no.

Philip pulled a book of matches from another pocket and struck one against the cover. Nothing happened. Embarrassed, he tried a second match and it lit. In an attempt to look suave, he cupped his hand over the light and held it up for me. I placed my cigarette into it. It didn't catch.

"You have to put the cigarette in your mouth and suck it in," he informed me.

"Suck it in," I questioned, "is that like inhaling?"

I hadn't realized this action was essential and knew my parents would never have approved. Having both quit cold turkey in

1968 (although my mother immediately got hooked on Trident gum), my parents were staunch anti-smokers now and had warned me about how hard it was to break this terrible habit once you'd inhaled. I knew that with one puff I'd be doomed to a nasty addiction I couldn't possibly afford on my meager allowance. Even so, I did as Philip told me. The cigarette lit for a second and then went out.

"You have to inhale harder," he said, "like this" and demonstrated.

Philip took a good long drag and I watched as his eyes opened wide and he launched into a coughing fit. A really long and drawn-out coughing fit. The kind Rhonda Shafter, our ancient theater director, probably had when she was his age. I should have run in and summoned help since it looked like Philip was about to die, but if his parents were anything like mine he wouldn't have wanted them to find out what he'd done, so I gave it a little more time. After another long minute he stopped coughing, switched to gasping, and then, finally, caught his breath.

"Are you okay?" I asked. Then, with suspicion, "Have you ever smoked before?"

"Of course I have," he insisted. "That's why I coughed so much. I need to cut down."

"Yeah, me, too," I said, and snuffed mine out.

"Okay, stupid idea," Philip admitted. "Let me try another one. Can I kiss you?"

He'd asked first. I never expected this. I had no idea what to say. I mean, the answer was yes, but could I say it?

"Um . . ."

Just then, Stacie Hofheimer, wearing the pants I'd broken in for her on Katahdin, grabbed me by the shoulders and implored breathlessly, "Mrs. Rosen, when you see your grandson, tell him not to be a haberdasher," then ran off.

"Do you know what she was talking about?" Philip asked.

I did. I knew exactly what she meant. It was a line from one of my favorite movies. Philip and I looked around the corner and saw a whole group of junior counselor girls who'd formed a crowd at the base of a tall evergreen tree. One of them pointed toward the top. "Life is up there," the group's leader shouted. "And life always matters very much."

"*The Poseidon Adventure*?" Philip said. "I loved that movie!"

"Me, too. I've seen it three times."

(That's where my ten dollars of bat mitzvah money went.)

"J'ever read the book?" Philip asked. "In the book the kid dies."

"I know exactly the part where I'd die," I told him. "It's where they have to swim underwater to the engine room. Y'know, where Gene Hackman goes first, but gets stuck on some metal and only Shelley Winters can save him?"

"Of course. And look, I think that's the part the girls are up to."

Sure enough, sixteen-year-old Ellen Wasserman, the junior counselor who'd gotten impetigo first, was playing the Shelley Winters role.

"I guess I'm not the champion of the Women's Swimming Association anymore," she gasped.

I was so jealous, and not just because she got the good part. I was jealous of all these girls and their ability to burst into this impromptu performance inspired by a hurricane. Watching these girls joyously running around in the rain, I started to worry about a lot of things: that I would never be that clever, that I would never have such close friends, that I would never know how to have that much fun.

Between the Legacies and the Losers, I had thought I was one of the latter, but now I worried that I was my own group, only not a group at all, that I was, in fact, unique, the squarest of pegs, forever on the outside looking in. I'd spent much of this summer watching other people having a good time and now I feared I would never be more than an observer, doomed to living my life in the third person singular. Philip was still waiting to kiss me. I had to do this; it was now or never.

The movie and the kiss were cut short by a gunshot. It came from the rifle of Mr. Thornton, who lived across the street and ran the only other general store in town. On the borderline of Skowhegan and Hinckley, Thornton's was the store with the pornographic matchbook covers ("Strike here, baby") that all of the boys coveted. Fed up with the endless rain, Mr. Thornton was not about to spend another night cooped up in his little cottage with the white picket fence counting the droplets dripping down the gutters.

Unable to come up with a better diversion, he'd stepped outside, thanks to his right to bear arms, to see if he could hit the swinging "Skowhegan Junior High" sign. The fact that people were around was of no consequence. When the second shot grazed the sign and ricocheted off the tree, the few remaining Poseidon passengers abandoned ship and ran inside the gym. I ducked down in the wet grass to see if he'd nail it on the next shot.

"Mindy! Are you crazy? What are you doing?"

Philip was peering out from a nearby doorway, motioning for me to come back inside. A couple more shots rang out and then we heard a different sound.

"I think he's reloading," Philip called out.

"Are you sure?"

"Not really," he yelled. "What do I know about guns?"

Good enough. I ran for the doorway, slipping on the wet grass and inadvertently falling into Philip's arms, which might have been a good damsel in distress tactic for someone else, but I outweighed him by at least twenty pounds. I would never have planned this move.

We were lying on the floor together, in the threshold.

"Are you all right?" he asked.

"I'm kind of wet."

"That doesn't count."

"Then I'm fine."

Philip lifted his head and put his lips on mine, which, having never done this before, I had to assume was the beginning part of a kiss. I closed my eyes only to realize I had a desperate need to know if Philip's eyes were closed, too, so I opened mine to look. His were wide open. We were staring at each other, eye to eye, nose to giant nose, less than an inch apart.

If only I had paid more attention to the soap operas Grandma Gussie watched when she stayed with us. I'd always ignored the TV when her "stories" were on, dismissing them as dull and irrel-evant, unaware that I was only a few years away from college dorm life and that whole Luke and Laura thing around which a genera-tion of students would schedule their classes.

I was pretty sure you were supposed to keep your eyes closed, so what was he looking at? I couldn't bear to know, so I closed mine again. And then the tongue thing happened and suddenly I wasn't me anymore. I was Benjamin Franklin with the key and the kite, jolted by the discovery of electricity. Forget my bat mitzvah. This was "The Day," the day I became a girl with a boy-friend. My feelings of terror gave way to elation. I was making out with a boy. I was in the club at last.

And then, God help me, in the very next instant it all went horribly wrong. Perhaps I wasn't doing it right. Perhaps he wasn't doing it right. Because if we were, how come, when I thought about it, I wasn't enjoying it? Why was this not the amazing romantic thing I'd been conditioned to dream of ever since my first expo-sure to an animated movie with the princesses in the gowns who pined after frogs and swept floors for evil queens? Why was this even worse than slow dancing, unfulfilling and unpleasant and reminding me of something else, of something repulsive, of that

time we visited my parents' friends in Morristown and their schnau-
zer, Cleo, licked the inside of my mouth?

I opened my eyes again to look for the answers. Was this what
kissing was? Was this how it was supposed to go? Thirteen and a
half long years for this? I may as well have been waiting for the
Great Pumpkin.

Why is nothing ever what it seems it should be, I wondered, *and
how much longer do I have to keep this up?*

This was what I wanted to know: When will this end? This
kiss, this unpleasant moment, this whole hideous adolescence? *Will
it always be this way? Will I always be this way? Are you there, Judy
Blume? It's me, Mindy. Hello? Is this thing on?*

Philip drew back and looked at me with a contented smile.
He had no idea we were not in the same moment, the same time
and place, maybe not even on the same planet. He stood up and
motioned for me to follow him inside, but I waited until he was
well ahead, to make it look like we weren't walking in together.

Back inside the gym the slow dancing continued. Dana was in
Aaron's arms and he was whispering something in her ear, the kind
of thing I would never hear if I couldn't grow up and handle being
close to a boy. I envied their maturity as I made a beeline for the
girls' room, to hide, entering in time to see nursing student Gita
Isak remove the stitches from Mindy Plotke's head with the twee-
zers from her Swiss army knife.

The hurricane was a washout, never reaching a dangerous level,
but there were floodwaters. They came from Dana Bleckman. Aaron
had not been whispering sweet nothings; he'd been breaking the
news to Dana that he had a girlfriend back home. This was just a
summer fling to him, meaningless and now over. "I hate him, I
hate him!" Dana wailed. "Oh, God, I love him, how could he do
this to me?" I understood her turbulent back-and-forth emotions
only too well, except that mine were all self-inflicted.

Jim Norbert dropped by early the next morning to let us know our camp was safe and no damper than usual. It was time to go back, to pack up our stuff, to attend one last campfire so we could say our farewells and then leave for good.

It occurred to me that we hadn't seen Saul Rattner since we'd arrived at the junior high. Perhaps he'd gone back and stayed at camp, prepared to face disaster, the way Captain Leslie Nielsen went down with the *Poseidon*. Or maybe he and the Mrs. had hightailed it into Bangor, rented a suite at the Hilton, and gotten drunk on champagne, paid for with our parents' hard-earned dollars. In any event, he had not endured the hardships of the night at the gym.

On the van ride back, a couple of junior counselor girls started up the theme song from *The Poseidon Adventure*. Yes, they were right, "There's Got to Be a Morning After," but the morning after this one I'd be heading back to New Jersey.

to the tune of
"Did You Ever See a Lassie?"

"It vas vinter in the valley green
And the vind blew 'gainst the vindowpane
And the vomen in the vaudeville
Wrote vilosophy from the vestibule"

17

THERE ARE COMPETING THEORIES ON HOW BEST TO PACK A TRUNK. Back at Camp Cicada, in the mountains of New York, there were rules for everything from the moment you arrived to the moment you left. They even had rules for how to pack, enforcing a method of rolling clothing into cylinders and pressing the pieces together side by side. The problem with this system was that my mother had shown me a different way—her way—a complex method of layering, ingenious in its Tupperware-like ability to burp out excess air. If I packed my mother's way, the inspecting Cicada counselor would have dumped out my trunk and made me start over. If I packed their way, I risked my mother's wrath upon arriving home. For the last two summers I'd opted for the wrath. I didn't have to worry what the Kin-A-Hurra packing rules might be.

"Just shove it all in," Autumn Evening yelled out. "Jump up and down on it until the stupid thing closes."

"What if the trunk breaks or my foot goes through the top?" asked Hallie. "It's only made of cardboard."

"We'll tie some rope around it," Maddy said, packing up the one flashlight she hadn't lost. "That's what I did last year."

This was the Camp Kin-A-Hurra way of doing things: whatever makes everything fit.

Dana didn't want to go to Boys' Side that last evening for the closing campfire, but Maddy and my bunkmates insisted it just wouldn't be the same without her. There was a lot of concern that she wouldn't be able to bear seeing Aaron one more time, that she wouldn't be able to handle the despair and anguish brought on by his betrayal.

No one had any idea that I, too, was terrified of attending the campfire, of having to see Philip, having to avoid him, or, worse, having to explain why I hid from him the night before, after our kiss. No one knew there was a good chance that on this last night of camp, we would test the theory of whether someone could actually die of embarrassment.

"Dana, we need you to sing," Autumn Evening insisted.

"But if you want to stay back," I offered, "I'd be happy to keep you company."

Dana sighed, "No, I'll go."

A real trouper, she slung her guitar over her shoulder and marched down the front porch steps for one last journey around the lake.

A final surprise was waiting for us when we got to Boys' Side. On this last night of camp we would be inaugurating a new campfire site. Our few past campfires had been held behind the maintenance shack, in a clearing in the woods, with a view of some old rakes and tractor parts. But this new campfire site was beautiful, a patch of empty land situated on the water's edge with an unobstructed view across to Girls' Side. It was the site where the Wolverines' bunk had stood. Made sense. We already knew stuff could burn here.

The way I saw it, I had two choices for how to spend the evening. I could head straight for the campfire to see if there would be marshmallows or anything else with s'more potential, or I could hang toward the back and try to glide unnoticed into the Boys' Social Hall or the dining hall or anywhere I wouldn't be spotted until the whole thing was over. I didn't see Philip so I went with a third choice: first looking for food and then thinking about hiding.

The fire burned against a backdrop of the most perfect sunset we'd seen all summer as Jacques and Wendy announced it was time for the annual awards presentations. "The first award," Wendy called out, "is for Worst Hiking Accident." This went to Mindy Plotke who hobbled forward to accept her prize, a gold spray-painted box of Pep cereal. Chip Fink won for Most Mosquito Bites. Biggest Hair was a tie between Ellen Byron and Howard Nemetz, and the Wolverines were announced as Worst Dressed After the Fire. All of these announcements were met with some applause, some razzing, and some general ennui. "And now," said Wendy, "the last award goes to Mindy Schneider."

I couldn't tell if my heart stopped or was beating ten times faster. What was I being singled out for? Biggest Nose? Worst Kisser? Most Unimproved Camper?

"This," Wendy said as she motioned for me to stand, "is just for you. A combined swimming and softball trophy we like to call 'Best *and* Worst Athlete'."

There was some applause and some razzing and some general ennui as I walked up toward the campfire to accept my prize.

"Thanks a lot," I sighed with relief as I accepted my still-wet gold box of old cereal.

This was definitely something I could live with, and at my father's suggestion I would later include the "Best" part on my thirteen college applications.

So delighted was I by this recognition that I momentarily forgot I was on the lookout for Philip. I plunked myself back down in the midst of my bunkmates and we cheered on Dana, who was next on the program. Despite her pain, she confidently strode up to the campfire and led us through a bunch of songs, all designed to reduce to tears as many girls as possible. Carole King's "Been to Canaan" succeeded. I'd never understood this back at Camp Cicada, teenage girls bawling their eyes out like they'd had the time of their lives and would never see each other again. Camp Cicada and its myriad of rules were oppressive—what was there to miss? And it's not like they couldn't get together during the winter. Those horrible girls all lived within fifteen minutes of one another in the Five Towns section of Long Island. "See you at camp next summer"? How about, "See you at the mall in Great Neck next Saturday." But here at Kin-A-Hurra, with campers and counselors from across the country, from around the world, it truly was possible we were saying good-bye forever.

As the younger girls were herded toward the parking lot and older girls stuck around for a few last good-byes, four of the waiters got up to sing a capella, to the tune of "Sloop John B":

> *"We come on the old Fer-ry/All my bunkmates and me*
> *'round Rattner's camp we did roam . . ."*

Couples were making out. Mostly they were quiet and romantic and the rest of us tried to look like we were listening to the waiters, but it was a pretty good show and hard not to watch, which is why I didn't see Philip approaching.

"So you think you'll come back next summer?" he asked.

"Um, I don't know."

I honestly hadn't thought about it.

Word came that the Green Truck had broken down by Saul's house, so the rest of us would be returning to Girls' Side via the Ferry. "Down to the waterfront," Wendy called out. Wendy wasn't crying. She still had four more days here, four more days during which she'd help the maintenance staff clean up after us. Now that should've made her cry.

Philip walked me down to the dock, never once questioning what had happened the night before. He'd been so patient with me all summer, as if he knew our time would come. This was the moment to kiss him first or let him know it was okay to kiss me. Instead, I shook his hand. He was still looking down at his hand as I stepped onto the Ferry, the waiters carrying on with their serenade:

> *"Get me out of this rain/This camp is insane*
> *I need to throw up*
> *I want to go home"*

Sailing away from the dock, watching Boys' Side grow small and distant, I was certain I would forever remember this as the summer I could have had a boyfriend and failed. And yet, as the Ferry carried us across the lake, both away from and into a memory, I could already begin to feel that warm glow of nostalgia.

Dana and I were the last ones still awake that night. "Want to go down to the lake?" she asked. All summer long, Dana had practiced a secret midnight ritual that everyone knew about. She'd go down to the water's edge, flashlight in hand, and send Morse Code–like signals across the lake to Aaron. Tonight, however, she'd make no attempt, knowing full well there'd be no reply. Instead, we sat down on a rotted bench adjacent to the grimy old aquarium that housed some unfortunate, captured catfish.

"You're so lucky," she said, starting to sob.

"Me? Why?"

(I had no idea how to console her, my excuse for keeping the conversation centered on myself.)

"You didn't need a boyfriend," she explained. "I mean, you could have had Philip, this cute, great guy who chased you all summer and never gave up, but you never took it seriously. You didn't waste your whole summer like I did. You were just here to have fun. Wish I could be more like you."

It would have been rude to ask her to repeat that.

"Something smells fishy to me," I said.

It was the aquarium.

"We should let them go," Dana said. "We should scoop out those fish and set them free."

"You mean touch them?" I asked. "Gross!"

"You just spent eight weeks in the armpit of Maine. Now you're getting picky? Come on. Stick your hands in. Stop being afraid."

As we scooped out the fish and tossed them back into the water, I could feel my own heart growing lighter with each little *plop plop plop* of liberation. Dana was looking out over the water, looking for that beacon of light from Aaron that would not be forthcoming. Only a full moon shone down on the lake, softly illuminating Boys' Side, as the last embers of the campfire burned themselves out. Everything always looked better from across the lake.

"So you think Philip's cute?" I ventured to ask.

"Kind of cute," she said. "And, like, he'll keep getting cuter. What? You don't think so?"

I didn't know what I thought anymore.

"Well, he's not like Aaron or Kenny," I said.

"Blech, be glad," Dana answered.

"What, you mean like he has inner beauty stuff or something?"

"No!" Dana laughed as she reached for one more fish. "I'm not trying to be deep. I just think he's kind of cute, in a goofy kind of cute way. Oh, forget it, if you can't even tell."

Actually, I'd probably known that about him all along; I'd just needed to hear it from someone like Dana, from someone who didn't have to say it.

The tank was now empty.

"I'm gonna miss those fish," I said.

"Please," Dana snorted. "They'll be here next year, just as big and smelly as ever."

And so would Philip. And if my parents could afford it I'd be back, too.

Everyone was in a big rush the next morning. Everyone had to be at the airport in Bangor by six a.m. Everyone but me. Hallie found an entire Hefty bag of clean laundry we'd forgotten to sort and we hurriedly divvied it up and stuffed the clothing into our duffel bags. One piece remained unclaimed. It was the world's largest pair of underpants and they didn't have a name tag.

"Oh, those are mine!" Autumn Evening called out. "I was quite obese in the 1760s."

"No way, I found them first," said Hallie.

A tug-of-war resulted in them both climbing in.

"Get out of my underpants!" Dana shouted, already recovering from her loss and running over. "Two is company and three's a crowd!" she shouted gleefully as she stepped in.

"Are you making fun of my big panties?" asked our counselor, grabbing hold of the waistband.

"Oh, for God's sake," said boring Betty Gilbert as she made her fifty-sixth (and last) black mark on the wall. "Those are mine!" and she climbed in.

Everyone was inside them now and only I was left.

"Come on, there's room," said Hallie, waving me over.

"We need you in the left leg," added Autumn Evening.

"C'mon!"

"Let's go!"

"I've got a plane to catch!"

"Hurry!"

Arms wrapped around one another for balance, the monster in the underpants ambled toward me. There was no escaping. I had to try. Trembling, I stepped in, knowing that fabric could stretch only so far. "Let's walk to the door," Dana suggested. "On the count of three. One, two . . ."

We'd taken only one step when, of course, the underpants ripped and we all landed on the floor in one big laughing heap. But right before that happened, for just a second there, I fit in.

*"till stars no longer gleam
until our youth has become a dream"*

Finish here

I GREW UP IN A FAMILY THAT WAS SO STRICT AND HAD SO MANY RULES it made life crazy. Then I went to a place that had no rules at all and somehow it made perfect sense.

Camp Kin-A-Hurra doesn't exist anymore. Something to do with the board of health. Maddy and Jacques bought Saul's house with the intention of coming up every summer, but after one season without campers it just wasn't the same. Only Jim Norbert remained on the property with his wife, Hendrika Devenpeck, one of Saul's unpaid foreign counselors in the summer of '76, who found Jim and the camp and all things American just dandy. As a wedding gift, skinflint Saul gave them two full acres of land perched atop a hill where Jim built a house forever overlooking "A Place to Watch." Thankfully, the rest of camp was not bought up by a developer and turned into a mall. Instead, it was given to the state of Maine and designated a park. Most of the buildings had to be torn down, though. Even the Point is gone.

In the spring of 1997 a reunion was held for anyone and everyone who had ever spent a summer at Camp Kin-A-Hurra. There was speculation for months over who'd show up, who'd married whom, and what everyone had become. Mindy Plotke and counselor Bobby Gurvitz were the only married camp couple from my era, having gotten together years later when they ran into each other at a Weight Watchers meeting in Manhattan. Everyone else had gone their own separate ways. Dana Bleckman became a high school music teacher, Hallie Susser a municipal court judge. Betty Gilbert returned to camp for eight more summers before becoming a professional fund-raiser. Her newest charity, the Saul Rattner Memorial Fund, helps send kids to camp. Autumn Evening Schwartz lives year-round in a former summer bungalow colony. As far as the local board of education knows, her three young children are being homeschooled, but, really, they're just sort of unschooled. Kenny Uber lost his money in a pyramid scheme. Philip Selig is a plastic surgeon.

I ended up with someone who never went to camp. Most reunion attendees left their spouses at home, knowing full well they just wouldn't get it, this thing we once belonged to, this cult we can never leave.

Altogether, more than five hundred former campers, counselors, and staff members gathered at Lake Wally one last time, representing thirty-one states, eleven foreign countries, every year of the camp, and the feeling that we'd all been in on something.

Acknowledgments

SURE, IT'S MY NAME UNDER THE TITLE, BUT IT TOOK A VILLAGE TO write this book.

I am indebted to the following people for stepping into the Wayback Machine with me to share camp anecdotes and/or photographs: Donna Rosenthal, Mitzi Saul, Susan Cohen Butler, Wayne Charness, Miriam Wagenberg Flatow, Stuart Alexander, Jonathan Bauer, Marci Auerbach, Gail Rubman Goldstein, Lisa Heyman, Cari Lorberfeld, Lisa Freedman, Michelle Schaffer, Jeffrey Berger, Bonnie Klaus Guttenplan, Shaily Steiner Hamenahem, and Kinereth Gensler. Thank you for helping me remember and for having made it worth remembering.

It's good to have friends who can read and write. The following people answered questions, provided advice, and, in several cases, slogged through various and sundry drafts. (Sorry about the sundry ones, and) thank you to: Gita Isak, Kathy McCullough, Sue Thornton, Billy Robertson, John Mitchem, Meg Hughes, Lynn and Peter Bernhardt, Susan and Howard Nemetz, Nancy Mansfield, Sierra Mansfield, Ellen Byron, Ellen Wasserman Goldstein, Kate Shein and Garrett Soden, Greg Fitzgerald, Stacie and Marc Moss, and the San Pedro Seven.

Additional thanks to Leeza Taylor, Bob Leventhal, and Glen Herskowitz for their patience and help with scanning, cropping, and editing the photos, and to my brother Jay for all that tedious Internet research.

As if it wasn't enough to make my friends read the early drafts, I also consulted several professional editors along the way. Thank you to Tristine Rainer, Michael Levin, and Susan Leon for helping me understand what it was I was writing and how to write it.

Thank you Carol Fitzgerald for not reporting my incompetence to Personnel that summer I temped in your office at *Mademoiselle*, and thank you for going on to create Bookreporter.com and for mentioning my manuscript to Dan Lazar at Writers House.

Thank you Dan for reading my book and offering to represent me at record speed and then sending it along to the perfect editor.

Thank you Lauren Wein, my editor at Grove/Atlantic, for hating camp and loving my book and making this really happen.

Thank you to my family for allowing me to use our real names and to my mother, Marylin, and my late father, Zachary, who, in spite of our seemingly impoverished circumstances, always scraped together the money to send me to camp. Sorry, Mom, the publisher wouldn't go for putting your name on the cover instead of mine even though everyone knows I couldn't have done this without you.

Credits for Photos Not Taken by Mindy Schneider